Wine Myths, Facts & Snobberies

∾

Techniques in Home Winemaking
The Comprehensive Guide to Making
Château-Style Wines

Kit Winemaking
The Illustrated Beginner's Guide
to Making Wines from Concentrate

Wine Myths, Facts & Snobberies

~

81 Questions & Answers on the Science and Enjoyment of Wine

Daniel Pambianchi

Véhicule Press

Published with the generous assistance of the Canada Book Fund
of the Department of Canadian Heritage.

Cover design: David Drummond
Technical editors: Arthur Harder and Dr. Ariel Fenster
Set in Minion and Filosofia by Simon Garamond
Printed by Marquis Printing Inc.

LIBRARY AND ARCHIVES CANADA CATALOGUING IN PUBLICATION DATA

Pambianchi, Daniel
Wine myths, facts & snobberies : 81 questions & answers
on the science and enjoyment of wine / Daniel Pambianchi
ISBN 978-1-55065-283-3
I. Wine and wine making—Miscellanea.
I. Title. II. Title: Wine myths, facts and snobberies

TP548.P36 2010   641.2'2   C2010-9000779-4

Published by Véhicule Press, Montréal, Québec, Canada
www.vehiculepress.com

Distribution in Canada by LitDistCo
www.litdistco.ca

Distributed in the U.S. by Independent Publishers Group
www.ipgbook.com

Printed in Canada on 100% post-consumer recycled paper.

About the Author

Daniel Pambianchi is the founder and CEO of Cadenza Wines Inc. and GM of Maleta Winery in Niagara-on-the-Lake, Ontario; Technical Editor for *WineMaker* magazine; a member of the American Society for Enology and Viticulture, the American Wine Society, and the Society of Wine Educators; and author of *Techniques in Home Winemaking: The Comprehensive Guide to Making Château-Style Wines* and *Kit Winemaking: The Illustrated Beginner's Guide to Making Wines from Concentrate.*

You can follow Daniel Pambianchi's work on his website and blog at http://www.TechniquesInHomeWinemaking.com/blog/ and on Facebook by becoming a fan of Techniques In Home Winemaking.

∾

Disclaimer

This book contains commentaries related to the science of wine, including winemaking, wine tasting, and wine and health. It offers opinions, presents scientific and medical research, some conclusive and some inconclusive, and expert knowledge from academia, the wine industry and literature. However, the information contained herein should not be construed as professional advice for the diagnosis or treatment of faulty wines or health problems; readers should always consult with qualified enologists for winemaking advice or medical doctors for any matter related to wine and health.

Neither the author, nor the publisher, nor the editors assume any responsibility for the use or misuse of information contained in this book.

Contents

Acknowledgements

This book spans several fields of science, some perhaps not so scientific; nonetheless, it involves consultations with and reviews by many, many experts, from winemakers to microbiologists and chemists to nutrition experts and neurosurgeons. I wish to specifically acknowledge the tremendous support of, and technical reviews by, Arthur Harder, a consulting winemaker to wineries in the Niagara region in Ontario and head winemaker at Maleta Winery; my chemistry professor and French wine aficionado Dr. Ariel Fenster from the Office for Science and Society at McGill University in Montréal, Québec; and Dr. Eric L. Gibbs of High-Q, Inc. who relentlessly crusades for PET bottle technology. I am also indebted to my dear friend Angela Campbell who meticulously reviewed the manuscript, and Fred Couch whose photography and photo-editing experience was invaluable. And of course, this project would not have been possible without the continued support of Simon Dardick and Nancy Marrelli, publishers of Véhicule Press, and their team. To each and every one and all my readers, and in the name of knowledge and good health, I raise a glass of (good) wine and say Thank You.

Preface

◟

WINE IS A FASCINATING SUBJECT. With its rich history dating back more than six thousand years and wine's current cultural status as a "higher" and healthier beverage, it is fraught with tradition, myths, beliefs and snobberies that span how to farm vineyards and grow grapes, how to make wine, how to serve it, and the health benefits of drinking wine—some are true, some aren't, and some are plain unbelievable, bordering on laughable.

With our knowledge of natural and pure and applied sciences, we can now explain and demystify traditions and snobberies, and debunk myths and beliefs. We certainly don't have all the answers on what is a very complex subject, but we can postulate reasonable hypotheses.

The objective of this book then is to provide commentaries, based on this scientific knowledge of wine, on facts, myths and snobberies encountered in our everyday interactions with wine. The commentaries are based on questions often posed to me as part of my work in the wine industry, notably during wine tours and tutored tastings, and my own curiosity that have lead me to research topics.

But be forewarned; many opinions and beliefs, whether scientifically proven or emotionally charged, are controversial. And so it is with this fascinating art of anything and everything that is wine.

So pour yourself a glass of wine, sit back, and enjoy the read; you may want to keep the bottle close-by.

About Wine-speak and
Scientific Terminology

∾

WINEMAKING—what some call *viniculture*—and the wine business have been greatly influenced by Europeans, particularly the French, who have developed an extensive wine vocabulary. To a large extent, French, Italian, German, Spanish and Portuguese terms from these Old World wine regions are still used in their original native language within New World wine regions while others have been translated. But some European words are often more accurate in their original language or simply cannot be translated; the best example is the use of the word *terroir* (see page 13 for the definition) for which no other language seems to have an appropriate translation to define the concepts. For these reasons, I have chosen to include such terms in their original language, in italics, and provided translations now commonly used in the English language. And because of the European influence on global winemaking, I provide all units of measures using the Metric system (also known as the International System of Units or *Système International d'Unités* (SI) in French) along with conversions to the U.S. system in parenthesis.

Likewise, every branch of science has its own specific terminology, language and form. In this book, I refer to any living organisms and microorganisms by their binomial names, in italic as is standard practice, according to current taxonomy (the classification of living organisms) rules. Binomial names are often derived from Latin or Greek words. On the first occurrence of a binomial name, the complete genus and species names are provided, and then the genus name is abbreviated as is usually done; for example, most wine yeasts belong to the species *Saccharomyces cerevisiae*, and is abbreviated to *S. cerevisiae*. Note that the genus name is treated as a proper noun, i.e., the first letter is capitalized, and the species name is treated as a common noun. It is often also more common to refer to organisms by 1) their species name only when the genus is understood—for example, winemakers talk about *vinifera* grapes in reference to *Vitis vinifera* grapes; or by 2) their more popular genus name when species are secondary—for example, winemakers refer to the yeast responsible for imparting a barnyard smell to wine as *Brettanomyces* in reference to *Brettanomyces bruxellensis*.

And there is also a lot of chemistry involved in understanding wine science. Here too, terminology can be overwhelming as various names are used by laypeople, winemakers, scientists, and professional agencies to describe the same compound; for example, what we all know as *vinegar* is commonly referred to as *acetic acid*, although it is also known as *methanecarboxylic acid* and *ethanoic acid*, as defined by IUPAC (International Union of Pure and Applied Chemistry) standards. IUPAC names tend to be more descriptive of the actual molecular structure and can be more useful in certain contexts. Here, we use a combination of both common and IUPAC names as usage varies between winemakers, wine chemists and enophiles.

Wine and Winemaking Science

~

ALTHOUGH WINE HAS BEEN MADE since the early days of civilization, some six thousand or more years ago, winemaking is still largely considered an art as the science of winemaking only started taking shape in the second half of the nineteenth century.

Winemaking, the art, is steeped in tradition in Old World wine regions, mainly western European countries with France having the most influence with their concept of *terroir*. Terroir refers to the amalgam of vineyard location, soil composition, microclimate, viticultural and winemaking practices all interacting to produce wine specific to the region or even to a vineyard parcel and which cannot be replicated anywhere else—or what some define as a "sense of place."

Winemaking, the science, was really born in 1857 when French chemist and "microbiologist" Louis Pasteur (1822–1895) proved that yeasts were in fact living organisms and that these were responsible for what he termed *alcoholic fermentation* in the production of wine from grape juice. Pasteur's new theory was in sharp contrast to Dutch naturalist Antoni van Leeuwenhoek's (1632–1723) hypothesis that yeasts were not living organisms, which he first observed two centuries earlier in 1684 using a microscope he had developed.

In post-Prohibition years, Americans and immigrants that had settled in the U.S. at the turn of the twentieth century rekindled interest in winemaking and re-launched the wine industry in America. However, it was not until the second half of the century that significant scientific research and development took place in New World wine regions such as the U.S. and Australia. In the nascent globalization of wine, the New World spearheaded technological changes fueled by a strong desire to make better wines akin to the best wines of France and to become world players in a fast growing market.

Enology, the science and study of winemaking, has since progressed tremendously to provide an ever-increasing understanding of the complex chemical reactions that not only transform grape juice into wine but also involve the causes of many kinds of spoilage. A friend once remarked that winemaking had become too "clinical," referring to the extensive use of science and laboratory analysis at the expense of the art. Perhaps so, but I believe in scientific progress, and particularly in winemaking where ultimately the goal is in understanding wines better and making better wines.

In this section we examine various aspects of viticulture and winemaking to understand what science has revealed and snuff out myths.

How is wine made?
Can you make wine from fruit other than grapes?

THE SCIENCE OF WINEMAKING, or enology, involves a blend of some very interesting chemistry, biochemistry and microbiology—some simple, some complex.

Wine is a fermented beverage, which means that sugar in grapes is converted to alcohol, more specifically to ethanol (ethyl alcohol), under the action of the enzyme zymase produced by wine yeast in a process called *fermentation*, or *alcoholic fermentation* to be more precise, as there are other kinds of fermentations.

In the traditional definition, wine is made from grapes but any kind of fruit or other non-grape juice that contains natural or added sugar that is fermented can be called *wine*, although these are generally referred to as *fruit* or *country wines*.

Wines of international renown are produced from grapes belonging to the genus *Vitis* and the species *vinifera*, often referred to as European species. *Vitis vinifera* includes several thousands of cultivars (short for *culti*vated *vari*eties) such as Chardonnay, Riesling, Sauvignon Blanc, Pinot Noir, Cabernet Sauvignon, and Merlot. Cultivars can also consist of many clones—varieties derived by vegetative propagation from a single mother vine variety. For example, there are as many as sixty Riesling clones in Germany to meet the needs of the different growing conditions.

To make wine, grapes are first crushed or pressed, or both, to extract juice so that it becomes exposed to indigenous yeast or cultured *Saccharomyces* yeast—most often, *S. cerevisiae*—added by the winemaker. Grapes may be whole-berry pressed to minimize tannin extraction in making certain styles of whites and particularly sparkling wines. Grapes are also destemmed—that is, the stems are removed mechanically and immediately discarded—to minimize extraction of harsh tannins. Stems can impart a very bitter and unappealing "green" taste to wine. We will explore tannins in more depth throughout this book.

As the yeast metabolizes sugar, alcohol is produced with carbon dioxide gas as a major by-product along with a whole host of other by-products responsible for the multitude of aromas and flavors and general structure of wine. Approximately two parts each of ethyl alcohol and carbon dioxide gas are produced for each part of sugar fermented.

In red winemaking, grape solids are left to macerate, or to steep, in the juice; that is how red wine gets its color—most grapes have "white" juice—as well as tannins and a host of other polyphenols. In white winemaking, there is no maceration; the juice is pressed off from whole or crushed grapes and immediately fermented without any skin contact.

Once fermentation is complete—that is, all the sugar has been converted into alcohol—the wine is stabilized with sulfite (a common preservative used in the food and beverage industry) to prevent microbial spoilage and further processed for commercialization before bottling. For example, the wine may be processed to ensure no ill-effects if stored at cold or hot temperatures; it may also be filtered for added clarity, or sterile filtered for added protection against microbial spoilage.

Natural or artificial additives that alter aromas and flavors are generally not allowed in commercial wines. In many winemaking regions of the world, acidity and sugar adjustments are allowed as well as the addition of oak products, such as oak chips, to impart oak aromas and flavors. Premium wines can also be aged in oak barrels to add further complexity, a traditional practice that is universally accepted and permissible. (Home winemaking is not regulated and, therefore, there are no rules; any additive is permissible to create any desired style of wine).

Once the wine is fully stabilized, it is bottled either for commercialization (for drinking) or for further aging in the case of premium wines.

Although our knowledge of the science and chemistry of wine

has advanced enormously, winemaking is to a large extent still considered an art deeply imbedded in tradition. Considering the many underlying chemical, biochemical and microbiological processes that must be controlled when possible, and the plethora of grape varieties, yeast selection, styles and blends of styles, and kinds of wine faults to deal with—just to name a few factors—it is easy to see why winemaking is indeed still an art or what Harry Paul refers to as the "*Gesamtkunstwerk* of winemaking" in *Science, Vine, and Wine in Modern France*. (*Webster's Third New International Dictionary* defines *gesamtkunstwerk* as "an art work produced by a synthesis of various art forms [as music and drama]".) However, art should not stand in the way of progress. It is only through our better understanding of the science that we can make better and better wines.

~

Do you crush grapes with your feet?

PERSONALLY, NO; however, the practice is still common in small wineries in Portugal where grapes are foot-trodden in *lagares*—the traditional crushing and fermenting vats.

The mention of crushing grapes by foot immediately conjures up images of bon vivant winemakers linked arm on shoulders frolicking in vats à la Lucille Ball in her memorable grape-stomping scene from *I Love Lucy*. Although the practice has some merit it can no longer be done economically in large wineries, where for example in Portugal, traditional *lagares* have been replaced by fully automated ones that replicate the gentle action of human feet.

Grapes need to be crushed very, very gently to minimize bruising the delicate fruit and extracting harsh tannins from seeds and stems. Actually, all that is required is to split the berries to expose the flesh and juice to be able to initiate yeast fermentation. Pressure exerted by the human foot is just right; it can split and crush grapes ever so

Fermentation tank area in a state-of-the-art winery.
Courtesy of Hidden Bench Vineyards and Winery.

Traditional grape stomping by foot.
Courtesy of IEEE Transformers Committee; photograph by M. Jaroszewski.

gently. Leo Loubère wrote in *The Red & the White: The History of Wine in France and Italy in the Nineteenth Century* that the "hardheaded vignerons [of nineteenth-century Côte-du-Rhône winemaking region] argued that the human foot, since it was soft and arched, could never crush the grape seeds and release an oil injurious to wine." Our winemaking forefathers were quite clever in spite of their lack of scientific knowledge, but their theories on gentle crushing still serve as the basis of modern research and practice. Much research on the optimal distance between crushing rollers and material used in manufacturing these has gone into designing and developing crushers that emulate the gentle pressure of the human foot.

And, yes, if you do decide to tread grapes by foot, your feet need to be sanitized and free of any disease.

~

How important is yeast selection in winemaking?

AFTER GRAPE QUALITY, WINEMAKERS—except those who rely on indigenous (wild) yeast—will agree that yeast selection is one of the most critical aspects of making a great wine true to its varietal characteristics. But choosing the "right" yeast, or more precisely, the right yeast strain, requires knowledge of yeast strain physiological characteristics and a flair for winemaking art.

Traditionally, wineries with estate-grown grapes relied on indigenous yeast for fermenting juice into wine. The microflora of vineyards is laden with many kinds of yeasts that can initiate what is called a *spontaneous (alcoholic) fermentation* when allowed to come into contact with the crushed grapes or pressed juice. Wineries with a long winemaking history and which have controlled their vineyards' microflora through self-sustaining viticultural practices will argue that this is the traditional and most natural way of fermenting. Newer wineries and those buying grapes from growers simply cannot rely on indigenous yeasts, most of which are spoilage yeasts, or which can impart off-flavors, or are simply not capable of fermenting wine to dryness. These yeasts may stop fermenting when the wine has barely reached four percent alcohol, for example.

In modern winemaking it is standard practice to use a yeast strain chosen from the more than one hundred strains available in dry format. The juice or must is first lightly sulfited to inhibit spoilage microorganisms; this also inhibits indigenous yeasts that may impart off-flavors. The dry yeast is then activated by rehydration and pitched into the juice or must.

The vast majority of wine yeast strains belong to the *Saccharomyces cerevisiae* (*S. cerevisiae*) species which have been isolated from various winemaking regions of the world and each has its own very specific organoleptic, or aromatic, and flavor characteristics. Each strain is recommended for specific grape varieties, wine styles and fermentation environment. For example, a strain isolated in Burgundy, France would typically be recommended for making a full-bodied Pinot Noir, the wine synonymous with Burgundy; whereas another strain, such as the well-known Lalvin EC-1118 (which some consider a *S. bayanus* while others a *S. cerevisiae*, hence the use of the more precise subspecies descriptor *S. cerevisiae bayanus*) might be used not for a specific variety but rather where fermentation conditions might prove difficult, such as when making sparkling wine, ice wine, or when dealing with a stuck fermentation. The physiology of the EC-1118 strain allows this yeast to withstand high osmotic pressure, to ferment in a much larger temperature range and to ferment up to eighteen percent alcohol at a fairly fast rate.

Whether you are making a full-bodied Cab, a buttery, oak-aged Chardonnay, or a fruit-packed Gewürztraminer, there is a yeast strain that might just make it easier to make that elusive wine.

Can wine be manufactured in the lab?

WHILE ATTENDING A WINE appreciation class, an inquisitive student asked if wine could be manufactured in the lab. "Yeah, sure," said the teacher without missing a beat, but offered no further explanation. It was quite a disappointing response; one which seemingly reduced wine to a simple, matter-of-fact drink. What a great missed opportunity to educate!

The teacher was nonetheless correct—you could theoretically make wine in a lab but practically an almost impossible task.

Wine is a very complex beverage; it consists of thousands of simple and complex organic and inorganic compounds, many of which have not yet been identified although Ted Rieger states in the May–June 2009 issue of *Vineyard and Winery Management* that "[r]esearchers believe that most of the chemical compounds in grapes and wines that contribute to aroma and flavor have now been identified." Organic compounds include alcohols, acids, polyphenols, sugars, esters, amino acids and amines, vitamins, minerals and aromatic compounds which all contribute to the positive aromas and flavors found in wine, as well as other organic compounds such as aldehydes and thiols that impart off-flavors or cause spoilage. These compounds are synthesized in the grapes during the growing and ripening cycle and can be created during fermentation from selected yeast strains as well as from winemaking operations such as barrel aging. Inorganic compounds such as potassium and calcium are derived from the soil and nutrients therein.

These compounds all exist in varying concentrations from the measurable to trace amounts and in countless combinations and permutations, all a function of the plethora of grape varieties, differences in viticultural practices and factors. Some factors are soil and climate, and kinds of yeasts which make the concocting of wine in the lab an impossible task.

An interesting question, indeed, but why try and reduce such a mystical beverage to some lab-concocted potion? Um, I think I'll go have a glass of wine to ponder this further.

Why do winemakers add sugar to their wines?
Is that not illegal?

THE PRACTICE OF SUGARING (adding sugar to grape juice or fermenting wine) is called *chaptalization*, so named after late-eighteenth-century French chemist Jean-Antoine-Claude Chaptal (1756–1832) who under French ruler Napoleon Bonaparte advocated this practice for increasing alcohol content in weak and unstable wines deemed too low in alcohol to provide "punch." Grapes did not always ripen to their full extent or some grape cultivars did not produce sufficient sugar to make wine with the amount of alcohol that was desired. After all, more likely than not, the physiological effects of alcohol is what men were after back then. Sugaring was the solution. The amount of sugar in juice determines the potential alcohol level— that is, if all the sugar is converted the wine achieves its maximum alcoholic strength.

Although the practice dates back to the eighteenth century— some claim that as early as Roman times a sweetening agent was added to sweeten wine, not to increase alcohol—the subject of chaptalization has stirred a lot of controversy. Ironically, it is the French who today claim that adulterated wine is not wine and that one should not interfere with tradition, particularly, when it comes to wine. *Oh! Quelle horreur!* Having said that, chaptalization is a necessity in winemaking regions of the world where a cool climate or when a poor growing season might not allow full ripening of grapes. A short growing season or a cool or rainy summer limits the amount of sugar produced in grapes. Wineries, which rely on profitability to stay afloat and pay off their huge capital investments, have no choice but to chaptalize, and in these times of global markets and competition, financial performance trumps tradition. Just ask the French who are witnessing dwindling sales from global competition in export markets.

So sugar is fermented into wine, but why do we talk about glucose and fructose? Are these not the same?

THE WORD SUGAR REFERS to the general class of carbohydrates—organic compounds made up of carbon, hydrogen and oxygen—that impart sweetness to food and drinks. Examples of sugars include sucrose (table sugar), lactose found in milk products, and glucose (dextrose) and fructose (levulose) found in fruits. Glucose and fructose are monosaccharides; this means that these simple sugars cannot be split any further. When joined together, these two monosaccharides form the disaccharide sucrose. Yeast cannot metabolize the sugar in chaptalized fermentation where winemakers add sucrose to increase alcoholic strength; the sucrose is first hydrolyzed by invertase enzymes into its monosaccharides in equal proportions—that is, sucrose is split into its two monosaccharides.

The distinction between glucose and fructose becomes important considering that fermentative *Saccharomyces* (*S. cerevisiae*) yeasts used in winemaking are glucophilic, meaning that they favor glucose over fructose, and therefore ferment glucose at a faster rate. A wine fermented to dryness—that is, the wine has less than 2 g/L (0.2 percent) of residual sugar—will therefore have less residual glucose than fructose. Any glucose and fructose remaining in the wine at the end of fermentation contribute to residual sugar. However, fructose is roughly sixty percent sweeter than glucose and so if two wines have the same residual sugar concentration, the one with more fructose will taste sweeter.

These behavioral differences demonstrate the effects of molecular structures. Glucose and fructose are isomers—that is, they have the same chemical formula but atoms are arranged differently and exhibit different behaviors.

~

I am new to winemaking, and I realize the importance of protecting wine with sulfite, but I am completely confused on the chemistry. Can you explain?

THE CHEMISTRY OF SULFITES has to be one of the most frustrating and confusing topics for novice winemakers.

The chemistry of sulfites involves simple concepts of ionic solutions. There is, however, a caveat: there is no universal agreement on what specific component of sulfite that protects wine with much on-going research trying to elucidate this topic. Here is what we know.

The role of elemental sulfur and its gas form sulfur dioxide (SO_2) is well known in viticulture and winemaking applications but the role of the various forms of SO_2—molecular, free, bound, and total—must also be considered to take effective preventive or curative actions in the cellar.

SO_2 is most often conveniently sourced from a sulfite salt, usually potassium metabisulfite, more commonly referred to as simply *sulfite* or *KMS*, which delivers approximately 57 percent sulfur dioxide by weight. SO_2 readily dissolves in water to form an equilibrium solution between the molecular form of SO_2, and sulfite and bisulfite ions. The equilibrium is highly dependent on the pH of the solution. As pH changes, the total concentration of molecular SO_2, sulfite and bisulfite ions remains steady, but the component concentrations increase and decrease to maintain the equilibrium. The higher the acidity of the solution (i.e., the lower the pH), the higher the concentration of molecular SO_2, the higher the alkalinity (i.e., the higher the pH) the higher the concentration of sulfite ions, and at midrange, the concentration of bisulfite ions is highest.

Winemakers most often refer to *free SO_2*—which represents the total concentration of molecular SO_2, sulfite and bisulfite ions—as the component that provides protection, although it is believed that the molecular form is what specifically protects wine against microbiological spoilage, but much research is still ongoing to determine which is most inhibitory. Molecular SO_2 enters microbial cells through their cell membranes and disrupts key microbiological functions. But given the diversity of microbial cell physiology, antimicrobial effectiveness of molecular SO_2 varies according to species as well as physicochemical factors, such as temperature and alcohol. This enables winemakers to use sulfite for selectively inhibiting or annihilating unwanted microorganisms (e.g., bacteria and non-*Saccharomyces* yeast) or enzymes while not affecting desirable *Saccharomyces* yeasts when added at the recommended sulfite rates.

In wine, the pH is generally in the range 3.00–4.00 and therefore, the equilibrium consists mainly of molecular SO_2 and bisulfite ions. These will react, or bind, with the many other organic compounds, such as acetaldehyde and phenolics, and become bound, and no longer provide protection. Total SO_2 is the sum of free and bound SO_2. Free SO_2 and total SO_2 are measurable parameters using aeration-oxidation techniques, and molecular SO_2 can be determined empirically. Governmental food inspection or controlled appellation agencies impose legal limits for commercial wines; for example, in the U.S., the limit is 350 mg/L (parts per million, or ppm).

White wines generally require more sulfite because they inherently have less protection compared to reds, which contain plenty of protective polyphenols, against oxidative reactions. Note that yeast fermentation produces a small amount of free SO_2—and so totally sulfite-free wines are not possible. Are there not yeasts that produce no SO_2? Not yet, but this is an interesting area of DNA and genetic engineering research. The future of this research seems very promising considering how much this field has progressed: The *Saccharomyces cerevisiae* yeast was the first eukaryote whose genome was fully sequenced (in 1996).

∾

Is the word *unfiltered* on wine labels a good thing or is it simply a marketing gimmick?

THE VAST MAJORITY of commercial wines are meant for early consumption, short cellaring, and most are introduced to the marketplace soon after production. Consumers expect such wines to be clear and free of any sediment; therefore, wine must be processed to ensure stability for a reasonable period of time.

Processing involves clarification by fining or filtration, or both. Fining involves adding an agent that hastens flocculation and precipitation of particles responsible for cloudiness; the wine is then racked (separated) from its sediment. There are various kinds of fining agents that precipitate particles through some form of chemical attraction. The condition of the wine and the winemaker's preferred choice of a fining agent generally dictate which is used (see page 27).

Filtration involves passing the wine through a filter medium to mechanically remove suspended particles. Increased clarity is achieved by successive filtering through media of different porosity. Some winemakers believe that this physical treatment of wine removes key aromatic and flavor compounds, and therefore diminishes quality. An unfiltered wine is thought to be of superior quality—or at least that is their belief—and should command a much higher price.

Because these wines cannot be sterile filtered, which would require pre- "quality-affecting" filtration, the wines are produced under very strict environmental controls in the winery to minimize any risk of contamination that could cause microbial spoilage.

So is this truly an issue of quality or is it merely a marketing tactic? You decide.

～

I have heard that egg whites have been—and still are—used for processing wine. Really? What for?

EGG WHITES ARE ONE OF VARIOUS SUBSTANCES, referred to as *fining agents*, used for clarifying wine and which have long been used in winemaking.

The primary role of fining agents is to clarify wine but they can also be used for fine-tuning color (not to be mistaken with clarity), particularly in whites, as well as aromas, flavors, and mouthfeel. They do so by combining with target particles, or colloids, by one of various actions, such as electrostatic or hydrogen bonding, so that the combined, heavier agent–colloid complexes settle out by gravity. Once the fining action has completed, the fining agent should completely settle out of wine, remaining in only trace amounts if any, and should not impart any odors or flavors. In that respect, they should be inert; however, that is always a challenge and never a guarantee. The choice of fining agents depends on the intended application, such as clarification, enhancing color, removing tannins for a smoother mouthfeel, and whether making red or white wine. Another important consideration is the need for fining agents and all wine additives to be "natural" or not be derived from animal by-products so that the wine qualifies as organic or vegan.

Fining agents are derived from various sources including proteins, such as albumin, gelatin and other collagens; clays, such as bentonite; silicon dioxide substances such as kieselsol; polysaccharides such as Sparkolloid (a proprietary formulation) and gum arabic; and synthetic polymers such as polyvinyl-polypyrrolidone (PVPP)—a polymer of polyvinylpyrrolidone (PVP), a water-soluble polymer made from the monomer *N*-vinyl-pyrrolidone and which has a long list of varied uses from medicine and pharmaceuticals to industrial applications. For example, it is used as a binder in many pharmaceutical tablets, as a stabilizer in food, and as a thickening agent in tooth whitening gels.

Proteins are polymers consisting of a myriad of amino acids

containing, among others, the elements carbon, hydrogen, nitrogen and oxygen, and are characterized by carbonyl groups which can easily bond to hydroxyl groups in phenols, such as tannins. (Carbonyl ($-C=O$) groups have a carbon atom double-bonded to an oxygen atom; hydroxyl ($-OH$) groups have a hydrogen atom bonded to an oxygen atom.) The resulting bonded structure becomes heavy and therefore causes the intended precipitation.

Egg whites are rich in albumin and belong to the class of protein-based fining agents, and have long been used for clarifying wine particularly oak-aged reds where they remove harsher tannins yielding a softer impression for a smoother mouthfeel with minimal impact on aromatic compounds. Egg whites are first mixed into an aqueous saline solution—in commercial winemaking the salt is typically potassium chloride as sodium chloride (table salt) is often not allowed—to avoid cloudiness due to globular proteins in the egg whites, which would be counter to the objective, and then added directly into the red wine. Globular proteins are much more soluble in a dilute saline solution than in water. But winemakers better have access to willing and able chickens as up to eight egg whites per standard 225-liter (60-gallon) barrel are needed. Wineries can have several hundreds or thousands of barrels!

Speaking of albumin, you may be interested to know that some countries still allow the use of blood albumin for fining wine but we will not describe that one here. It is not acceptable and its use is illegal in North America.

Gelatin is derived from collagen, an insoluble fibrous protein found in skin, tendons and the bones. As positively charged gelatin particles easily bond to negatively charged tannins, gelatin must often be used in conjunction with kieselsol, or silica gel, an aqueous solution of silica dioxide. Gelatin is widely popular in kit winemaking because of its clarification effectiveness and ease of use. It also finds applications in softening astringency in whites that may have a little too much of a bite.

A close relative of gelatin is casein, a protein found in milk of mammals. Casein can excessively strip wine of color, and for that reason, it is often used only for reducing the brownish color in whites afflicted with slight oxidation.

Isinglass is a very pure form of gelatin prepared from the air bladders of sturgeons or of other fishes. Isinglass is very effective, less finicky in its use, and has little affinity for tannins—as opposed to the other protein-based fining agents—and so it often used for kit winemaking.

Bentonite most commonly in the form of sodium bentonite is a moisture-absorbing kind of clay, often of volcanic origin which is widely used as a fining agent in both commercial and home winemaking because it is very effective in clarifying as well as stabilizing against proteins that can cause wines to become cloudy, and is also allowed in organic and vegan wines. Bentonite is particularly recommended for treating whites given their much-lower phenol content and higher risk of protein haze that can cause wine to go cloudy. Fining occurs when the negatively-charged bentonite molecules attract to the positively-charged protein molecules.

Polysaccharides, as the name implies, is a polymer of many saccharides joined together. Cellulose, the structural material found in wood and plants is a well-known example of a polysaccharide consisting of a long chain of D-glucose saccharides. In winemaking, alginates such as the well-known proprietary Sparkolloid formulation derived from algae are popular polysaccharides used for fining.

Gum arabic is another multi-purpose polysaccharide; it consists primarily of arabinose, a pentose sugar. This one is really interesting, so let's take a closer look. Gum arabic may not be as popular in winemaking, although it has many applications: It is widely used in food and beverage processing not only as a stabilizer but also as syrup for making soft drinks, gummy candies, and chewing gum. Gum arabic is a natural gum extracted from specific species of African

Acacia trees and made into a colloid dispersion of saccharides and glycoproteins. It is recommended for rounding out tannins in reds, for increasing mouthfeel in both whites and reds, and for increasing persistence of bubbles in sparkling wines. It can also be used to enhance the action of metatartaric acid in cold stabilization (see page 106) by encasing tartar crystals thereby keeping them completely separated and inhibiting tartrate crystal growth. It can improve aromatic intensity and complexity as well as "palate" balance or to stabilize red wine color pigments in young wines by acting as a protective colloid that aids in preventing pigment precipitation. It reduces tannin astringency as well as increases the perception of body or volume, and reduces the perceptions of acidity and tannin harshness while adding body. In bottled red wine, it stabilizes color and hinders their precipitation, prevents ferric casse (an iron disorder that causes wine to become cloudy or hazy) in high-iron content wines; and enhances *perlage* or bubbling in sparkling wine. That is a very diverse set of nifty applications.

PVPP is effective in absorbing and precipitating "small" flavonoid phenols responsible for browning in wines as well as excessive bitterness. Precipitation occurs when the oxygen atom of the carbonyl groups in the high-molecular-weight PVPP molecules form a bond with the hydrogen atom in the phenols' hydroxyl group.

～

Are wines made from kits any good?

ABSOLUTELY!

Judging from competition results, kit wines are excellent, increasingly often undistinguishable from commercial wines, and are winning more awards.

Kit winemaking has come a long way since concentrate-in-a-can wines of yesteryear. Today's kit wines are produced from either high-quality concentrate or a blend of concentrate and juice sourced from premium vineyards from around the world.

Wine kit production technology progressed significantly over the last decade which has improved the quality of concentrates and the resulting wine and, obviously, it involves some interesting and sophisticated chemistry.

Kit manufacturers source grapes from vineyards from around the world in both northern and southern hemispheres to have a constant supply throughout the year. Concentrates are produced year-round, unlike winemaking in each specific region which happens only once a year. Kit winemakers can therefore make wine year round.

But like growers and wineries, kit manufacturers also harvest grapes based not only on sugar level, acidity, and pH, but also on physiological and sensorial (organoleptic) characteristics such as color and flavors which must be balanced with the chemistry of the grapes.

Once harvested, white varietal grapes are crushed and pressed and the juice is transferred to tanks to allow unwanted solids to settle. The juice is stabilized with sulfite and then enzymes are added to break down pectin and bentonite, both of which play a critical role in clarifying the juice as well as, ultimately, the wine. The juice is further stabilized at very cold temperatures where it is then separated from the heavy deposit at the bottom of the tank and filtered. The juice must be maintained cold to prevent fermentation from starting on its own.

In the case of red varietals, where color must be extracted during the juice processing stage (as opposed to during fermentation in winemaking), grapes are crushed and allowed to macerate with the juice in a tank at cold temperatures to prevent fermentation from starting on its own. Special enzymes are added to extract color and aromas from the grape skins; this is the most critical step in producing red juice of high organoleptic quality. When the desired quality is achieved, the grapes are pressed and the juice is moved to the next stage of processing. Some grapes may be kept for shipping with kits where additional maceration is desired during winemaking.

The white or red juice is run through a concentrator to remove some of the water content and concentrate the juice. Key aromas and flavors, which may be lost during processing, are recovered and returned to the concentrate; this is the critical step that now ensures minimal loss of aromas and flavors compared with kits of yesteryear. The concentrated juice is then tartrate-stabilized by chilling to hasten precipitation of tartrates—harmless, colorless crystals—to ensure that this does not happen during winemaking or while bottles are chilled in the refrigerator.

At this point, the manufacturer decides on the quality and style of wine the kit is intended to produce. The concentrate may be blended with other concentrates to replicate, for example, a Bordeaux-style red (typically a blend of Cabernet Sauvignon, Cabernet Franc and Merlot), or varietal juice is added for greater varietal character.

As a last step, the concentrate is pasteurized to eradicate any latent spoilage microorganisms, and is then packaged for sale.

Home winemakers then effortlessly transform the kit into excellent wine according to the chosen style in a matter of a few weeks.

~

Why are wines vintage dated? Does it really make a difference?

THE QUALITY OF A WINE is primarily determined by the quality of the grape-growing season. Yes, you also need a good winemaker, but you still need good grapes and good grapes need warm days and cool nights with very little water to grow healthily with just the right balance of sugar, acidity and flavors. But no two seasons are alike— one season might be perfect, another may have seen a lot of rain (which could possibly cause grape bunch rot), while others may have been affected by a hailstorm at harvest time. All these factors contribute to quality; for example, in a rainy vintage, grapes will accumulate excessive water which, in turn, will dilute aromas and flavors and cause an imbalance between sugar and acidity. This then becomes the winemaker's challenge—making good wine from a poor vintage. As the laws of economics dictate there will be a much smaller demand for lesser quality (often with higher volumes because of the increased yields from rain), prices will be significantly lower than in a superb vintage. As an illustrative example using a First Growth wine from Pauillac (Bordeaux), the 2005 (98) vintage of Château Mouton Rothschild sells for $965 in Québec, Canada, while the 2001 (90) vintage will set you back $550 and the 2004 (89) vintage a mere $490. (Numbers in parentheses are *Wine Spectator*'s vintage ratings out of 100.) Vineyards were blessed with a superb summer and perfect growing conditions in 2005 for making rich, full-bodied wines, albeit in small quantities. In 2001 a cold September gave rise to more medium-bodied wines with higher acidity while in 2004 a bountiful crop coupled with excessive rain and cooler temperatures produced plenty of lighter wines.

You be the judge.

~

People often speak of *balance* in wine. What does that mean exactly, and what does an unbalanced wine taste like?

WHEN WE DRINK WINE, we expect all elements to be in balance and to complement each other for a desired style. If any one element dominates, the effects of the other elements are diminished causing the flavor profile and wine to be unbalanced. For example, excessive, hard tannins would be unsuitable for an early-drinking, fruity red wine. Unlike a cup of coffee where one adds milk or sugar, or both, to taste, wine is produced in bulk and cannot be adjusted in every serving. The wine must be produced in balance according to its intended style. Beyond that, it comes down to a matter of taste. For example, some people may be partial to red wine only and may not like sweet, dessert wine, while others may not enjoy sparkling wine.

Achieving balance in wine can therefore be a formidable challenge for winemakers. Consider all the vineyard management, winemaking, and cellaring factors such as weather, pruning techniques, fertilizer selection, maceration techniques, yeast selection, malolactic fermentation, oak-aging regimen, maturation period, and the myriad of other factors which can become overwhelming. Winemakers who purchase grapes or juice have no control over the quality of the raw material in producing a well-balanced wine.

There is no exact science or tools to guide winemakers in making well-balanced wines, but Émile Peynaud (1912–2004), who was a respected, leading research enologist and teacher of modern winemaking, best described guiding principles in achieving balance in his authoritative book *The Taste of Wine: The Art and Science of Wine Appreciation*:

> A wine tolerates acidity better when its alcoholic degree is higher; acid, bitter and astringent tastes reinforce each other; the hardest wines are those which are at the same time acid and also rich in tannins; a considerable amount of tannin is more acceptable if acidity is low and alcohol is high.
>
> The less tannic a red wine is, the more acidity it can support [necessary for its freshness]; the richer a red wine is in tannins [necessary for its development and for its longevity] the lower should be its acidity; a high tannin content allied to a pronounced acidity produces the hardest and most astringent wines.

We will see in section *Wine Service*, balance can easily be thrown off when paired with unsuitable food.

Aside from imparting oak aromas and flavors, why are wines aged in barrels considered superior to those from stainless steel tanks?

OAK, SPECIFICALLY WHITE OAK as it relates to wine, is a type of wood that is rich in "good" tannins, or more specifically, gallotannins and ellagitannins—as opposed to harsh, undesirable tannins found in grape seeds and stems—essential in shaping the structure and body of wine, defining its aging potential, as well as acting as a natural clarifying agent. Tannins contribute to mouthfeel, which can create a *puckery* feeling, akin to drinking cold tea. They are imparted through the simple contact of wine with wood and the extent of extraction depends on contact time; over-extraction would cause wine to become overly astringent.

The underlying barrel physics and chemistry responsible for the evolution and development of wine can be distilled down to an easy-to-understand explanation—the basic phenomenon is called *micro-oxygenation* or *microbullage* in French. Wood, being a porous material allows the barrel to "breathe" by allowing alcohol (ethanol) and water to evaporate to the outside and air to penetrate to the interior and oxygenate the wine. The tight but porous joints between stave and head segments hasten evaporation and oxygenation. Evaporation and wine absorption into the wood cause wine volume inside the barrel to decrease; the resulting headspace is known as *ullage*. Barrels must be regularly filled or topped up to replenish evaporated wine and to avoid over-oxygenation which would otherwise oxidize and spoil the wine. By keeping the barrel full, the infinitesimally small oxygenation (micro-oxygenation) is controlled and essential to the wine's development.

During the aging (maturation) period, micro-oxygenation softens tannins and increases bouquet complexity by allowing a very small amount of oxygen to interact with the wine's compounds and transform them into more complex aromas and flavors. In addition, oak aging—specifically, toasted oak—stabilizes pigments thereby

Vintage quality of top-estate Bordeaux wines dictates market prices; here, 2005, 2001 and 2004 vintages of Château Mouton Rothschild wines.

Fine wine aging in oak barrels.
Courtesy of Jackson-Triggs Vintners.

intensifying and stabilizing color. The inside of barrels is usually toasted over an open fire, which gives wines added complexity of toasted oak notes during the barrel-aging process.

But barrels come at a cost: They are expensive, ranging in price from US$500 to $1000 or more for a standard 225-liter (60-gallon) barrel. They must be properly maintained to avoid spoilage (of wine or barrel, or both), and can be used on average for three vintages before they need to be replaced, though some wineries extend their use up to five years, and perhaps more by shaving the inside to expose new wood and re-toasting the newly exposed wood over an open fire. There is a danger though in re-toasting shaved barrels: Wine penetrates sufficiently deep in the wood that wine alcohol too is toasted, resulting in off-flavors.

What are the alternatives?

Oak alternatives such as oak chips, cubes and staves are now widely used for crafting "oak-aged" wines at a fraction of the cost, are easier to use and will impart oak aromas and flavors very quickly but they do not provide the benefits of micro-oxygenation.

Does all of this really matter?

If you are partial to oaked wines in the $15 range for example, and which you do not intend to age, it certainly does not matter, but if you are a fine wine aficionado and expect that your prized bottles of top Bordeaux, super Tuscans and Napa cult wines will cellar for ten, fifteen, twenty or more years, then only the finest barrels will be used.

$\sim$

Is there a difference between American and French oak?

THERE IS A PLETHORA OF BARREL TYPES now available to winemakers with a choice of provenance of the wood, drying and seasoning methods, toast level and size, all of which impact price. A typical 225-L (60-gal) American barrel will cost approximately $500 versus $1000 for a typical French barrel.

Today, white oak is the wood of choice for winemaking, however, not all white oak is the same nor are all barrels manufactured the same way. First of all, there are various species of white oak within the *Quercus* (oak) genus, each having somewhat different characteristics. *Q. robur* is the most widespread species in Europe while its subspecies *Q. sessilis* and *Q. pendunculata* are most often used for French barrels and *Q. alba* is predominantly used for American and Canadian barrels which tend to impart more oakiness. Secondly, wood and barrels are processed and built differently in different countries. Methods used in drying and splitting or sawing wood, for example, can impart significantly different characteristics and consequently, oak species and manufacturing methods directly influence cost.

Such are the reasons why winemakers request barrels from specific countries, the most popular being French, American, and to a large extent, Hungarian oak barrels, although Eastern European and Canadian barrels are also available. It is also not uncommon to find French barrels manufactured using a mix of French and Eastern European wood, and in some cases, winemakers can specify provenance down to a region or forest, the most common being Allier, Limousin (*Q. pendunculata*), Nevers (*Q. sessilis*), and Tronçais. Each wood type has its own special characteristics or is preferred for specific wines. For example, Cabernets, Merlot, Bordeaux-style blends, and Pinot Noir are known to have an affinity for Nevers and Tronçais wood. Provenance can also be specified for American oak and includes areas or states such as Minnesota, the Appalachians, Kentucky, and Indiana.

Drying and seasoning methods used in preparing oak wood destined for barrels also play a significant role in the style and quality of wine. To make barrels more affordable, they may be manufactured from wood that has been kiln-dried—a quicker and cheaper production process—though this method is now seldom used in premium barrel manufacturing. Premium barrels are manufactured from wood that has been air-dried for two or three years, for example. The advantage of air-dried wood compared to kiln-dried is that the former imparts more subtle aromas and softer tannins to wine. Likewise, the longer the air-drying period, the better. For example, very young air-dried wood would impart undesirable green oak aromas and harsh tannins. Manufacturers of premium barrels usually provide a choice of two- or three-year air-dried wood, albeit, at different prices.

The type of toasting—burning the inside of a barrel over an open fire—is as important as the type of wood or drying and seasoning methods. It complements the wine by imparting another level of complexity to the bouquet and flavor profile not otherwise possible with oaking alternatives. Before barrel heads are seated onto the ends, open-ended barrels are placed over an open fire for toasting. The high toasting temperature acts on the wood components such as cellulose, hemicellulose and lignins, to soften tannins and release desirable aromas such as vanilla, caramel, coffee, chocolate, and aromatic sweetness.

Three levels of toasting are available based on the desired wine style: light, medium, and heavy. Usually, only the barrel staves are toasted; however, barrels can be ordered with toasted heads if extra *toastiness* (toasted notes) is desired. Next time you visit a winery and are lucky enough to be given a tour of the barrel room, see if you can identify the types of barrels used. You might find something like "3-YEAR MT-TH" inscribed on barrel heads; it stands for "three-year, air-dried, medium-toasted oak wood, including the heads."

~

Where do all those aromas and flavors that winetasters so eloquently speak of come from? Are winemakers allowed to add aromatic ingredients or artificial flavor?

FIRST OF ALL, NO; NO WINEMAKING REGION allows the addition of aromatic ingredients or artificial flavoring agents. It is strictly forbidden.

Aromas are very complex natural compounds created in the grape juice in berries during the growing season and particularly during the ripening phase. Some of these are said to be *bound* or non-volatile, and so we cannot initially smell them, but during winemaking, the compounds become *free* and volatile and can therefore be detected depending on concentration, volatility, and alcohol concentration.

Alcohol concentration, you ask?

Higher alcohol reduces surface tension thereby allowing some volatile compounds to shine through to a greater extent.

Could this explain the trend to higher alcohol levels in modern wines?

Other aromatic (and flavor) compounds are also created during fermentation where specific yeast strains can impart a broad range of aromas and flavors. We have already seen the importance of yeast selection on winemaking and more specifically, yeast produces glycosidase enzymes that break up glycosides (molecules in which a sugar is bound to a non-carbohydrate functional group) into its sugar component and a flavor-bearing molecule. So not all aromas exist in grape juice.

Here are some compounds and aromas commonly found in wine: diacetyl (butter), rotundone (black pepper), methoxypyrazines (bell pepper), 4-mercapto-4-methylpentan-2-one (passion fruit, cat urine [ever heard of *Cat's Pee on a Gooseberry Bush* Sauvignon Blanc?]), megastigmatrienone and zingerone (tobacco and spices), linalool (floral, citrus), *cis*-rose oxide (roses), ß-damescenone (apple, honey), and guaiacol and 4-methylguaiacol (smoky). Guaiacol and

4-methylguaiacol are specifically found in oak-aged wine where these compounds are the result of lignin (woody cell walls of plants) thermal decomposition during the oak toasting process.

Throughout this book, we will look at some very specific aromatic (in the olfactory sense, not necessarily in the chemical structure sense) compounds and their chemistry in wine.

∼

I always thought that I should ferment wine at cool temperatures to preserve delicate, fruity aromas but then I read that reds should be fermented relatively hot and as quickly as possible. Can you explain?

That's right! Both statements are correct. Ferment whites very slowly at cool temperatures and reds relatively hot and as quickly as possible. We only need to look at the general chemistry of aromatic compounds, alcohols, and phenols to understand why.

Aromatic compounds—those that contain benzene rings in their molecular structures—is the class of compounds primarily responsible for giving wines their fruit, floral and other kinds of aromas and flavors. Aromatic compounds tend to be very volatile and so high fermentation temperatures would volatize the compounds, robbing wines of their delicate aromas and flavors. Whites are more susceptible as the compounds are more temperature-sensitive and, therefore, low-temperature fermentation is usually recommended. It is also recommended for young, fruity reds meant to be drunk quickly.

In fuller-bodied reds, where more phenolic extraction is necessary to give the wines more depth of color and more tannin, winemakers need to juggle the opposing chemical processes of phenol extraction and alcoholic fermentation. Color pigments in reds are part of a group of phenolic compounds called *anthocyanins*, which are glycosides that are less soluble in alcohol, therefore, color needs to be extracted early during maceration and fermentation as the rate of extraction diminishes rapidly after the onset of fermentation. In a process called *cold soak maceration*, crushed grapes are often macerated at cold temperatures to hasten color extraction while inhibiting fermentation. During cold soak maceration and before fermentation begins, tannins are also extracted at an exponential rate though slower than color pigments, however, extraction continues at a reduced but still exponential rate during fermentation as tannins are more soluble in alcohol. In winemaking regions where grapes do not reach full color maturity because of the shorter and cooler growing season, a technique known as *thermovinification* is often used to extract more color by heating grapes to approximately 80°C (176°F). The extra heat disrupts cell structures in the grapes to release anthocyanins more readily and inactivates undesirable enzymes such as lacasse found in *Botrytis*-affected grapes (see page 79).

At Maleta Winery, we also perform a *post-fermentation cold soak* that can last up to three weeks which will "soften" the tannins and make wines more approachable in their youth.

~

My German friend tells me that the best, genuine Riesling wines should smell of petrol with some mineral notes. Is this true?

YES, HE IS RIGHT.

At Maleta Winery, Riesling is one of our specialties. The wine is made in both dry and off-dry styles from genuine Riesling grapes from relatively old vines planted in the late 1960s. After twelve to eighteen months of aging, the wines start to show their characteristic petrol or kerosene aroma, however, it is most discernable after three or more years. Visitors not familiar with Riesling are often taken aback by what they perceive as a fault; many people actually do not detect it. But to the Riesling connoisseur, the petrol aroma is the mark of a true and great Riesling wine. It may not necessarily develop in all Rieslings; it is usually not found in high-yielding vineyards but rather where yields are kept very low with grapes harvested at high acidity, and for this reason, these wines will typically command a higher price. The petrol aroma is much more pronounced—almost off-putting—in Riesling wines from hot-climate regions, and that is why Riesling is considered a cool-climate varietal.

So where does the aroma come from?

The compound responsible for imparting the pejorative-sounding petrol smell—what many of us consider an aroma and a positive attribute—is TDN, or 1,1,6-trimethyl-1,2dihydrona-phthalene if you really want to know and is the result of hydrolysis of the glycoside of 2,6,10,10-tetramethyl-1-oxaspirol[4.5]dec-6-ene-2,8-diol.

Did we mention that some of the wine chemistry would be complex?

Let's look at it from another angle. TDN is a compound that belongs to a special class of isoprenoids known as *norisoprenoids*, and is the result of the hydrolysis of carotenoids. The *isopren* part in *norisoprenoid* suggests that the compound is made up of isoprene (2-methyl-1,3-butadiene) units, the five-carbon, unsaturated (meaning it has two carbon–carbon double bonds) hydrocarbon compound found in rubber and terpenes. The *nor* part means that there are thirteen carbon atoms. Carotenoids are compounds made up of four terpene units and are therefore known as *tetraterpenes* which are also derivatives of terpenes.

You will most likely not remember the chemistry of the petrol aroma in Rieslings next time someone asks you, however, you will at least be able to explain that it is completely normal and that the wine was not fermented in old kerosene tanks.

~

Why do red wines age better than whites?

THE EASY ANSWER IS: POLYPHENOLS—those long, complex chains of phenols that are in great concentrations in red wines but not whites.

As we have seen, polyphenols which come mainly from grape skins during maceration in red winemaking and during barrel aging act as antioxidants to provide red wines with their age-worthiness in addition to other roles they play such as tannins, which provide structure.

But there are other physicochemical factors (assuming proper storage conditions) that influence age-ability including: alcohol, sugar, acidity, and pH, and whether the wine has undergone malolactic fermentation (see page 63).

In general, the higher the alcohol content, the longer wine can be cellared. Reds are typically in the 12.5 to 14.5 percent alcohol range while whites are in the 11.0 to 12.5 range. What favors white wines is the higher acidity which acts as a preservative. If the wine has high sugar content, such as in Sauternes wines—those lusciously sweet, age-worthy wines from the Sauternes appellation in Bordeaux, France—can last a lifetime. The rich sugar content creates a high osmotic pressure that acts as a preservative against a renewed fermentation or spoilage.

It is a misconception that all wines require aging. The vast majority are produced to be consumed as soon as they appear on store shelves and only ultra-premium ones are meant for cellaring. You will need to research wines, vintages, and producers to determine the aging potential and then you will need a cellar or space with proper environmental storage conditions.

~

Is there any significance to legs (tears) descending the inside of a wine glass?

REPEAT AFTER ME: "LEGS"—or the less chauvinistic "tears"—say nothing about a wine's quality.

When swirling a glass of wine, it is to volatize or release the myriad of charming aromas, to please our olfactory senses while tasting. That is absolutely true; but the tears that form and slowly trickle down the glass do not reveal anything about the "full-bodied-ness" or quality of the wine, though admittedly, they look very appealing. It is a misconception that tears are an indication of the amount of glycerol, and that the more glycerol, the more body the wine will have.

Body in wine is determined by the amount of phenols, namely tannins, alcohol and residual sugar—and not glycerol that is present. In general, a combination of high concentrations of any of these three will make a wine full-bodied such as a tannic, 14-percent alcohol red wine or a syrupy sweet Sauternes wine. Note, that contrary to popular belief, high alcohol alone does not make a wine full-bodied; you can have a 12.5-percent full-bodied red with lots of rich tannins and conversely, you can have a thin, though hot and heady, 14-percent red. That is why whites are usually not described as full-bodied, except for oak-aged Chardonnay.

Glycerol (glycerine) is a very viscous and sweet-tasting trialcohol—that is, it has three hydroxyl groups in its molecular structure—and is a by-product of sugar fermentation. Glycerol concentration is higher in reds because the amount produced is proportional to the amount of alcohol produced where reds have generally higher alcohol concentration than whites and because more is produced at the higher fermentation temperatures which are used in red winemaking. However, the concentration found in wines is below detection threshold and so it does not play a role in body and quality of wine.

Now then, when a glass is swirled, surface tension on the glass

45

causes the wine to *stick* to the surface. Ronald S. Jackson best explains the phenomenon in *Wine Science: Principles and Applications, Third Edition*.

> Tears form after wine is swirled in the glass, and a film of wine coats the inner surfaces. Because ethanol evaporates from the film more rapidly than from the main volume of wine, the surface tension on the sides of the glass increases, relative to that in the bowl. As water molecules in the film pull closer together, due to increased water activity, droplets begin to form. As their size increases, drops start to sag, producing 'arches.' Finally, the drops slide down, forming the tears. When the drops reach the surface of the wine in the bowl, fluid is lost, and the drops pull back. Once formed, tears continue to develop as long as alcohol evaporation pulls up sufficient wine to offset the action of gravity pulling the film downward. Cooling generated by alcohol evaporation further helps generate convection currents that draw wine up the glass.

This phenomenon can be demonstrated by a simple experiment using food coloring—keep in mind that food coloring contains propylene glycol, an alcohol. Pour a small amount of any wine into a wine glass; swirl it to allow the wine to reach as high up as possible on the inside surfaces; dump the wine out completely; and let the glass stand on the counter. As the tears form, pour in drops of food coloring—you will need about twelve drops in a standard INAO (Institut National des Appellations d'Origines, the organization for controlling wine production in France) tasting glass. Let the glass stand and watch as the alcohol moves up the sides of the glass to create a psychedelic mosaic.

So make sure to carry a vial of food coloring to your next wine tasting to explain that tears do not reveal anything and to demonstrate the phenomenon. You might be the hit of the party.

~

Why is vitamin C added to wine?

VITAMIN C IS NOT ADDED TO WINE as a vitamin supplement or physiological antioxidant (see section on *Wine and Health*) but rather as an antioxidant to protect the wine.

Vitamin C, best known as *ascorbic acid* to winemakers and *L-3-keto-threo-hexuronic acid lactone* to chemists is often used in home winemaking for its antioxidant properties, however, its use is not well understood.

Ascorbic acid only has an extremely transitory antioxidant effect on wines. It fixes to dissolved oxygen in wine and quickly converts to dehydroascorbic acid—a weak organic acid—and produces hydrogen peroxide, a powerful oxidizer. Therefore, adding only ascorbic acid can actually compound the effects of oxidation, and *must* be used with sulfur dioxide where sulfite ions react with hydrogen peroxide to form sulfate and reduce oxidative effects. Following this oxidation, ascorbic acid is exhausted and serves no further function. It is mainly used to scavenge oxygen in wine before bottling or other operations where the wine will be subjected to little temporary aeration.

Another function of ascorbic acid is preventing a condition known as *ferric casse* which is caused by oxidation of iron supplied from the soil and present in wine. Ferric casse will cause wine to become cloudy and hazy when there is a high concentration of oxygen (typically from excessive exposure to air) in high-iron content wines. Those handled with minimal exposure to air do not need to be treated with ascorbic acid. This is difficult for home winemakers to assess because there is no simple tool to measure iron content, however, ferric casse is a very rare occurrence nowadays because iron-rich equipment is no longer used for handling wine. Most equipment is now manufactured from food-grade plastic or stainless steel. As a reminder, avoid brass fittings on pumps, valves, hose attachments or any equipment that will come into contact with wine.

∽

What is phylloxera, which is claimed to have destroyed countless vineyards throughout the world in the late nineteenth century?

PHYLLOXERA IS A FAMILY of sap-sucking aphids that includes the grapevine-devastating root louse *Daktulosphaira vitifoliae* which is simply referred to as *phylloxera* in viticulture. (It is still often classified by its old scientific names *Phylloxera vastatrix* or *Phylloxera vitifoliae*.) Specifically, it attacks the rootstock to cut off the flow of water and nutrients to the vine.

Phylloxera is native to North America. It is believed to have been introduced into Europe and the Old World winemaking regions in the late 1860s when North American vines were imported to supplement the needs of growing vineyards and wineries; however, this spawned a worldwide phylloxera epidemic, ruthlessly ravaging vineyards from France down to Australia. In France alone, more than 2.5 million hectares (6 million acres) of vines were uprooted. This was on the heels of the ravages of powdery mildew, the leaf disease also known as *Oidium* caused by *Uncinula necator* fungus, in the 1850s. (The fungus spreads to grape clusters and causes secondary rot and off-odors described as moldy, earthy and mushroom-like.) North American grapevines, such as *Vitis labrusca*, were spared because these had developed natural resistance to phylloxera, however, *Vitis vinifera* grapevines—used throughout Europe in making world-class wines such as Chardonnay and Cabernet Sauvignon—had not. Interestingly, Chile's *vinifera*-planted vineyards were spared; it is not known why but it is suspected that the louse could not traverse the Andes Mountains from the east because it could not survive high altitudes nor cross the Pacific Ocean from the west.

The cause of the problem was not immediately apparent and was often misdiagnosed. Much research was undertaken to identify root causes (ok, the pun was intended) but this took very long. In the meantime, the louse spread across continents, continuing to inflict damage at a dizzying pace.

Many proposed remedies failed, and failed miserably. There was a glimmer of hope when Baron Paul Thénard, son of French chemist Baron Louis-Jacques Thénard (1777–1857) of hydrogen peroxide fame, applied carbon disulfide, a strong, poisonous and foul-smelling insecticide around the affected vines. The chemical was fairly effective against phylloxera, but it had two shortcomings in addition to being a very expensive treatment making it unsuitable as a long-term solution. First of all, carbon disulfide is very volatile and therefore was required to be applied in large doses. Secondly, it had to be applied annually which weakened vines and in cases of prolonged applications killed vines altogether. Other chemical warfare was proposed such as potassium xanthate and potassium sulfocarbonate to overcome the first shortcoming of carbon disulfide but again, these treatments were simply too expensive. There was also an attempt to use a very dilute solution of Sarin, an organophosphorus compound chemically known as *methylphosphonofluoridic acid 1-methylethyl ester*. The solution was applied to the soil around the vine trunk, and although it proved very effective, its use was considered too toxic and dangerous as an ongoing remedy. Sarin is a highly toxic nerve gas once used, for example, as a chemical warfare agent and in the 1995 Tokyo subway attack.

Vineyardists had become desperate, and desperate times called for desperate measures. Some resorted to voodoo-like solutions such as burying toads under the vines to dispel the evil forces but to no avail.

A couple of long-term solutions were finally identified. One solution recommended by Gustave Foëx (1844–1906) Director of the École d'agriculture de Montpellier involved breeding European *V. vinifera* cultivars with native North American species, however, these "French" hybrid varietals did not produce the same style and quality of wine that the Old World had become accustomed to with *V. vinifera* varietals. The second solution, now standard practice across the world in planting and replanting vineyards, developed by

British-born American entomologist Charles Valentine Riley (1843–1895) and French botanist Jules-Émile Planchon (1823–1888) in the late 1870s, involved grafting *V. vinifera* vines onto very specific North American rootstocks such as *V. riparia*; the result is a *vinifera*-yielding vine on a phylloxera-resistant rootstock.

Today, phylloxera is not as a serious threat, except in those vineyards and winemaking regions that persist on planting ungrafted *vinifera* grapevines and which have not been attacked yet or those vineyards that had been replanted with vines grafted onto still-vulnerable North American rootstocks as evidenced by the occurrence of phylloxera in California in the late 1980s. Specifically, in Napa and Sonoma counties, vineyards were replanted in the 1960s using a rootstock known as *AxR1*, or Aramon Rupestris #1, a cross between Aramon, a *V. vinifera* cultivar, and Rupestris, an American *V. rupestris* grape species but which have not developed total immunity to phylloxera.

Modern vineyards now have a wide selection of rootstocks known to be highly resistant to phylloxera and which can be adapted to the specific environmental conditions. One example is SO4 or Selection Oppenheim #4, a cross between two native North American species, *V. berlandieri* and *V. riparia* cultivars, known to perform well in cool-climate regions, particularly in wet soils.

Considering the cost of ripping vines out and replanting a vineyard, the fact that vines only produce wine-worthy grapes after five years, on average, and with its associated revenue losses, it is surprising that hardships of the past have not been deterrents to these vineyardists.

~

The phylloxera root louse devastated countless vineyards the world over in late 19th century.

Powdery or downy disease on roses is a sign of an impending grapevine disease.

Why are roses planted at the end of vineyard rows?

PLANTING ROSES AT THE END of vineyard rows is a simple and effective trick—what some call a miner's canary—as an early warning sign of an impending disease, usually powdery mildew or downy mildew because roses are more sensitive than grapevines. If either disease sets in, the vineyardist then sprays the vineyard with appropriate fungicides. Those who routinely include fungicides in their vineyard management practices do not need to plant roses.

Powdery mildew, also known as *Oidium*, is a disease triggered by the fungus *Uncinula necator* (or *Erysiphe necator*) that causes white powder-like spots on vine leaves and grapes during the growing season, particularly in microclimates of high humidity and temperatures and shade. If the fungus attacks berries, grapes can take on strong earthy (1-octen-3-one) and geranium-like [(Z)-1,5-octadien-3-one] smells, and can split and open and become prone to other diseases. But according to the *Journal of Agricultural and Food Chemistry*, research conducted at the Faculté d'Œnologie of the Université Victor Segalen Bordeaux demonstrated that the aromas were much attenuated as the compounds are enzymatically reduced by *S. cerevisiae* yeast during alcoholic fermentation. Powdery mildew can be easily prevented with a sulfur spray once (if) signs of the disease appear on the roses.

Downy mildew is a much more serious disease that is triggered by the mold *Plasmopara viticola* which thrives in more humid and persistently wet conditions. It causes "oily spots" on leaves or greasy yellowish spots that turn a brownish color. Infected leaves and affected grapes eventually drop from vines and can survive the winter and once again spread the disease the following spring. Downy mildew can be prevented with a copper sulfate spray solution once, and if, signs of the disease appear on the roses.

∼

Is wildlife in the vineyard a problem?

WILDLIFE IN THE VINEYARD is a big problem and a costly one at that.

Wildlife control is neither an art nor a science for vineyard managers although various solutions and devices have been developed. It requires determination and good physical fitness—wildlife often needs to be chased out of vineyards throughout the day. Stories of vineyard personnel spending the days around harvest in the field chasing wildlife are not unheard of.

Depending on geographical location and ecological emplacement, vineyards can be a feasting ground for jackrabbits, raccoons, deer, birds, and many other kinds of animals.

How serious a problem is it?

A flock of starlings can devour a small vineyard in almost no time, leaving unprepared vineyard personnel defenseless with no reaction time.

The problem starts at *véraison*—when red grape varieties start turning to a deep blueish-purple color and whites to a golden color, and grapes start losing that harsh malic acid and accumulate deliciously-sweet sugar. That is when defense mechanisms need to go up: programmable electronic propane cannons, or bird bangers, or other electronic "scarers," such as bird distress call scarers, handgun-operated bangers, crackers, and whistlers, decoys, such as falcons or eagles, dogs to scare away birds and other vineyard predators, netting draped over each row of vines to keep birds off grape bunches or electrical fences around the perimeter of the vineyard to keep deer out.

How effective are these mechanisms?

Bird bangers are no longer effective as birds seem to have become accustomed to the loud bangs; many vineyards in Niagara still use these devices. Bangers run on propane gas and are timed to fire several blank shots at regular intervals. Sure, birds get scared—so do unsuspecting people touring vineyards—then fly off to the neighboring vineyard only to come back minutes later. Handgun-operated bangers and crackers are costly and need to be manually fired at regular intervals by vineyard personnel, and so it is an expensive proposition. Decoys too have limited efficacy, and dogs, well, they tire after a while in the hot late summer, early fall sun.

Nets have proven to be very effective, but they are expensive. For example, a type of control netting requires that nets be draped over each and every row of vine and for the entire length which then need to be removed come harvest if mechanically harvesting using tractors. When harvesting by hand, nets can be left on vines until the start of the next season but this makes harvesting a painful chore.

Now, if I can only find a way to keep those two-legged critters of the children kind away and from pulling off those luscious grapes.

⌇

Why are the most successful winemaking regions of the world located near a lake or other major waterways?

To MAKE GREAT WINES, you need the best grapes possible and that is why *vignerons* will often assert that wine is made in the vineyard. Weather patterns (mesoclimate) in a viticultural area, quite often right down to a vineyard parcel (microclimate), play a determining role in the quality of grapes grown. Vines and grapes need a lot of sunshine and warm or hot days and properly tended with sound viticultural practices such as leaf-thinning, to expose grape bunches to the sun, and irrigation where there is not sufficient water to feed the vines.

It is no coincidence that France, Italy, Spain, California, Oregon, Niagara and British Columbia, South Africa, Chile and New Zealand, just to name a few, have exceptional grape-growing seasons for making world-class wines. One common denominator is that these regions are in close proximity to major bodies of water or waterways that provide ideal microclimate conditions for growing European

V. vinifera varieties.

During the hot summer days, not only are sunshine and high temperatures key drivers for photosynthesis but the body of water also absorbs and stores a vast amount of thermal energy (heat). As the sun sets and temperatures drop off, thermal energy stored in the body of water is transferred to the cooler mainland—remember that air flows from hot to cold—to provide a continuous source of warmer temperatures. During the winter months, this thermo-dynamic phenomenon is key in *viniferas'* ability to survive.

~

What is the impact of global warming on winemaking regions and the wine industry as a whole?

GLOBAL WARMING (or the more encompassing term *climate change*) is both a natural and an anthropogenic phenomenon (involving the impact of man on nature) responsible for the increasing average temperatures on the earth's surface and oceans over time. Impacts include warmer days and fewer cold nights, heat waves, droughts, erratic seasonal cycles, and other extreme weather patterns. According to the Intergovernmental Panel on Climate Change (IPCC), a United Nations Environment Programme (UNEP) and World Meteorological Organization (WMO) initiative, the increase over the last century has been 1.33°F (0.74°C).

The major anthropogenic culprits of climate change are stratospheric ozone depletion and emissions of carbon dioxide, methane, nitrous oxide, and ozone gases, which are mainly the result of anthropogenic activities such as fossil fuel use and agriculture. These gases cause the so-called greenhouse effect, first observed by French mathematician Jean-Baptiste Joseph Fourier (1768–1830) in 1824 but not quantified until 1896 by Swedish physical chemist Svante Arrhenius (1859–1927). The greenhouse effect is a phenomenon whereby radiation by gases trapped in the atmosphere cause warming of the earth's lower atmosphere, surface, and oceans.

The study and forecasting of climate change is a gargantuan scientific endeavor as it is based on very complex, highly-intertwined factors studied over long periods of time and on intricate modeling to predict future impacts. Though there is much debating in the scientific community—and the political arena—regarding the extent of climate change impacts and timing, one thing is for sure; climate change impacts are for real and the world must take prompt action to mitigate these.

How big of an impact is climate change on the wine industry?

Woods Institute for the Environment at Stanford University communications manager Mark Shwartz cites a 2006 study led by Noah Diffenbaugh, assistant professor of environmental Earth system science at Stanford which based on an analysis of historical temperature data from California, Oregon and Washington, concludes "that global warming could reduce the current U.S. wine grape region by 81 percent by the end of the century." Now that is some apocalyptic prediction!

Over time, man has planted and replanted grape cultivars best suited to regional and local climates. For example, it is well known that Pinot Noir best adapts in cool-climate viticultural areas for making premium wine. The effects of global warming and climate change would then transform cool-climate regions into subtropical regions and subtropical regions into tropical ones. Cultivars adapted to one type of region would no longer be able to thrive in a different climatic region. It would be akin to trying to grow Pinot Noir in Central America today. Grapes would develop increased sugar levels and a corresponding alcohol increase, reduced acidity that will create balance challenges but likely without a commensurate increase in flavor profile—flavor development takes time, not necessarily more heat. Then, vineyards would need to be replanted with better-suited cultivars—quite the expensive proposition, particularly considering that, on average, it takes five years for new vines to produce wine-worthy grapes.

Failing that, vineyards will be faced with many new viticultural challenges such as: a shorter growing season which may not allow grapes to develop optimum maturity for making premium wines, increased irrigation which entails higher water usage, already a scarce resource, and significantly higher capital and operating costs, and a whole host of new pests and diseases that will require new technology and means to fight.

Whole businesses may be seriously impacted. Consider the existing situation in Germany where making *Eiswein* (Icewine) year after year is not a given since the necessary winter conditions are not guaranteed. If there will no longer be cold winters, there will be no deep freeze to make those lusciously sweet nectars of the gods and growing grapes in Champagne for making high-acid wines for bubbly will also become a challenge. On the flip side, we could see wines—perhaps even premium wines—being produced from non-traditional wine producing areas such as the UK and Scandinavia.

Although wine regions throughout the world have embraced and are implementing sustainable agricultural and winemaking practices (see page 141), it behooves us all to become "greener" and support climate change mitigation measures—at least for wine's sake.

∼

While on a visit to Ontario's Niagara region I noticed so-called wind machines sitting high in the middle of vineyards. I was told that they are used for protecting vines during a cold snap. How do they work?

THIS IS A LESSON IN THERMODYNAMICS, and yes, in fact, the wind machines are used for protecting vines during cold winter days or a spring or fall frost.

European *V. vinifera* grapevines are not as cold-hardy as, for example, North American *V. labrusca* or hybrid vines and can die when the *dew point temperature* nears critical crop-damaging temperatures. The dew point temperature is the air temperature at which water vapor starts condensing and which takes into account relative humidity. The critical crop-damaging temperature for vinifera vines is around −20°C (−4°F) whereas cold-hardy vines such as Baco Noir can withstand temperatures down to −26°C (−15°F). Anything colder than that and one would wonder why anyone would want to grow vines and make wine in such cold weather.

In extreme winter cold areas where winemakers are determined to grow *V. vinifera* grapes in spite of the huge risks, vines are trained to remain short so that they benefit from the warmer temperature closer to the ground and so that they can be buried underground for the hibernating months. This is cost-prohibitive and impractical, as in the Niagara region or even California, given the large acreage planted to *vinifera* cultivars.

During the winter months, the most common vine-damaging phenomenon is *advective freeze* caused by the horizontal movement of a mass of cold air. Those vineyard sites situated on a steep incline, particularly if sloping towards a lakeshore or other body of water, such as on the Niagara escarpment or "Bench" high above Lake Ontario are better protected from advective freeze than low-lying sites on flatland areas, such as in Niagara-on-the-Lake. Incoming cold air flows down the incline and away from the vineyard to protect vines. This phenomenon can be clearly witnessed in such sites where, for example, the vineyard slopes northerly downwards; the northernmost part of the vineyard will look more damaged than the southernmost vines on the slope.

In the spring, if a morning frost sets in once vines have started budding, the buds may not survive and can cause a crop shortage like the 2005 vintage that the Niagara region experienced; some growers lost their entire crop from cold injury that year.

Cold injury from a late spring or early fall frost or a mid-winter cold spell can occur when there is a sudden large temperature drop

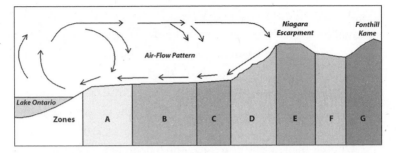

Airflow pattern due to the effects of Lake Ontario and the Niagara Escarpment over various zones: (A) lakeshore effect zone; (B) level plain between escarpment and lake; (C) base of escarpment slope; (D) steep north-facing escarpment slopes; (E) slopes above the escarpment; (F) flat and rolling land south of the escarpment; and (G) high elevation and equidistant between lakes (Ontario and Erie).
Courtesy of Ontario Ministry of Agriculture, Food and Rural Affairs.

Wind machines standing tall above a vineyard protecting vines against cold winter days or spring frost.

at ground level due to cold air moving in coupled with a vineyard's thermal loss. This phenomenon is known as *radiational freeze*; it causes warmer air from solar energy from the lower level to rise and create an inversion layer just above the vineyard—a condition of cold temperature at vineyard level and warm temperature just above. At a height of as little as 15 meters (50 feet), the air is a few degrees warmer.

Double-bladed, gas-powered wind machines are installed in the middle of vineyards to move that warmer air back down into the vineyard and cause *temperature inversion*. The blades spin in a slightly off-perpendicular plane (e.g., 6° angle) down towards the vineyard and rotate a full three-sixty degrees around the supporting tower. The few degrees difference (3°–5°C, or 5°–9°F) is all that is needed for vines or buds to survive. In fact, temperature inversion only works when the difference in temperature between the vineyard and the inversion layer is a few degrees. If the difference is constantly higher, then, perhaps, the site is not appropriate for planting *vinifera* cultivars.

In Niagara, wind machines have become ubiquitous. At a $30,000 per unit capital investment, wind machines are still the most cost-effective solution; one wind machine can cover approximately four hectares (ten acres). The machines operate only for the (expected) short duration of the cold snap. One drawback of wind machines is the high noise level, definitely a problem with neighbors particularly because the machines typically turn on at night.

Another solution is to install a "drain" device, also known as a *selective inverted sink* (*SIS*), developed by Uruguayan engineer Rafael Guarga in the late 1990s. One such device is the SHuR Farms Cold Air Drain®, which, according to their website, "selectively drains only the coldest air layer from the orchard/vineyard floor, expelling it upward 300 feet [91 meters], where it is dispersed into the inversion layer. The warmer air can then move down and replace the cold air." The technology is not unlike wind machines, however, the blades rotate in a horizontal plane parallel to the ground to displace cold air upwards.

Yet another solution to minimize the risk of radiational freeze during a morning frost is to spray a water mist over the vines using micro-sprayers for the duration of the frost. The water mist then freezes to release heat and protect the berries and vines.

In winemaking regions such as Napa Valley, California, where a cold snap or a spring frost is a less frequent occurrence, some vineyard owners have been known to call in helicopters to displace the cold air over their vineyards or to fire up huge heaters to protect vines from the cold. Again, these measures would be cost-prohibitive in Ontario's Niagara, though helicopters were used before the advent of wind machines, or New York's Finger Lakes regions where cold-weather patterns are highly probable, in spite of these areas being at the same latitude as northern California (check the map).

～

I have heard a lot about the use of new technology such as reverse osmosis and spinning cones. What are they used for?

OVER THE LAST DECADE OR TWO, the average alcohol level in commercial red wines has increased steadily, very often exceeding 14 and even 15 percent alcohol by volume. The trend is definitely to make richer, bolder, and higher alcohol wines.

Vineyardists are constantly "pushing the envelope" to try and harvest grapes with higher sugar levels by extending the hang time without compromising flavors or quality. This may not always be possible, particularly in cooler-climate winemaking regions or when high sugar development is unachievable under poor vintage conditions.

So how do the pros manage to churn out high alcohol wines even when grapes are harvested at sugar levels that yield "only" twelve percent potential alcohol? The answer: reverse osmosis—a very expensive technology that only big wineries can afford but few, if any, will admit to using. Interventionist winemaking is still seen as untraditional and therefore a shunned practice.

Osmosis is the flow of a solvent, such as water, through a semi-permeable membrane from the more concentrated solution to the more dilute solution until equilibrium is reached (i.e., both solutions have the same concentration) if the process is allowed to complete. In winemaking, osmosis would cause water to flow into the lower-density wine, and so the process must be reversed, hence *reverse osmosis*, also known as *nanofiltration*, where pressure is applied to the more concentrated solution to reverse the flow of water. Reverse osmosis (RO) can therefore be used for concentrating grape juice or wine by removing some of the water content. This will yield a higher-alcohol wine. RO can also be used to remove volatile acidity (VA) in tainted wine.

In winemaking applications, RO is implemented using cross-flow filtration technology where juice (or wine) is made to flow tangentially to the filter media—as opposed to perpendicularly across the filter media in typical clarifying filtration applications—to avoid clogging the media but it tends to be problematic with unclarified juices.

Before reverse osmosis, vacuum distillation techniques were used for concentrating the must by applying heat under vacuum, however, this caused flavor loss, some caramelization and browning caused by the Maillard reaction, i.e., a heat-enabled chemical reaction between amino acids and reducing sugars that causes non-enzymatic browning.

What if wine has too much alcohol? Can you not simply add water back, or what the French call *mouillage*, to dilute the alcohol content? Aside from being illegal in many winemaking regions of the world (it is legal in the U.S.), adding water which quite ironically is commonly referred to as *amelioration*, would also dilute aromas, flavors, phenolic content and color, acidity, and so on. Certainly not a good thing.

To complete the picture on modern technology and alcohol

manipulation, some wineries also use a spinning-cone column that uses centrifugal force and vacuum to reduce alcohol in wines when looking for better balance in the event that grapes have not ripened to their optimum level.

Although the above technologies may seem foreign, these are all employed by wine-kit manufacturers to produce their products used by home winemakers.

Another new "technology" gaining popularity with commercial wineries is encapsulated yeast which is becoming popular in the production of dessert or sweet wines. Its use is simple; encapsulated *S. cerevisiae bayanus* yeast is added to the must and then removed from fermentation when the desired residual sugar level is obtained. Since the yeast remains encapsulated and does not escape into the wine, there is less handling, and fermentation is easier to stop, resulting in superior wine quality. Encapsulation technology involves embedding the yeast in a calcium alginate shell that prevents the yeast from getting into the fermenting wine. The beads are placed in a nylon bag that is then inserted and suspended in the fermenting vessel. The bag is simply removed to stop fermentation at the point that the desired residual sugar is achieved. Clever!

∾

I had heard of malolactic fermentation, but ever more so now. Why?

THE ROLE AND BENEFITS of malolactic fermentation were only introduced into modern winemaking in the mid-twentieth century based on the research of enology pioneers Jean Ribéreau-Gayon and Émile Peynaud. (Jean Ribéreau-Gayon was the grandson of Léonard-Ulysse Gayon, who collaborated extensively in Pasteur's work, and father of Pascal Ribéreau-Gayon, another Bordeaux enology luminary.) Their work spawned a new area of research on the physical chemistry, biochemistry and microbiology of malolactic fermentation which has shed some light on this practice. However, we have only started scratching the surface, and while we wait for research to provide more answers, opinions on the benefits of malolactic fermentation and its process are abound with current-day winemakers.

Malolactic fermentation (MLF) is the partial or complete enzymatic transformation of naturally occurring, sharper-tasting malic acid (think green apples) into the softer lactic acid (think milk) induced by indigenous or cultured lactic acid bacteria, usually *Oenococcus oeni*. Carbon dioxide gas is a by-product of this transformation and which is allowed to escape prior to bottling. MLF is generally desired in high-acid wines to reduce total acidity, but it can also enhance the flavor profile and mouthfeel.

A partial and random MLF is what gave birth to *Vinho Verde*, the fizzy white wine produced in the Minho region of northern Portugal. "Vinho Verde" literally translates to "Green Wine" owing not to its color but rather to its youthfulness and tart taste. Today, MLF in Vinho Verde is allowed to completely transform to ensure the wine remains stable while in the bottle and until consumed and, instead, the wine is artificially carbonated just prior to bottling.

However, the most familiar result from MLF is diacetyl produced from pyruvic acid when glucose is catabolized. Diacetyl, or 2,3-butanedione, is a diketone that imparts buttery and nutty flavors in Chardonnay, however, if it is not managed properly it can spoil a wine outright.

Although the positive effects have been understood for quite some time, it is only recently that extensive research has shed light on the negative effects of a poorly managed MLF. For example, *Lactobacillus* bacteria can give a spoiled-milk taste to wine, while *Pediococcus* bacteria can give wine an oily texture and which produce a high level of diacetyl, giving wine an objectionable buttery or cheesy smell.

One area of ongoing research is the timing of malolactic fermentation—that is, should it be carried out before, during or after the alcoholic fermentation? On this point, there are more opinions than winemakers. There seems to be an irreconcilable divergence between academic research and experience in the cellar.

As we will examine in the section *Wine and Health*, MLF is implicated in the production of biogenic amines, which have known physiological effects.

~

What is lysozyme used for?

LYSOZYME IS A PURIFIED, freeze-dried enzyme isolated from egg whites used for suppressing lactic acid bacteria after malolactic fermentation and for achieving microbial stability. It is only effective on gram-positive bacteria (i.e., *Lactobacillus*, *Oenococcus* and *Pediococcus*); it is not effective against gram-negative bacteria (i.e., *Acetobacter* and *Gluconobacter*), spoilage yeasts, including *Brettanomyces*, or molds. It also does not have antioxidant properties, however, unlike free sulfur dioxide (from sulfite) lysozyme is most effective in wine at higher pH when spoilage lactic acid bacteria thrive the most. As such, it cannot replace the use of sulfite but can be used concurrently to reduce the amount of sulfite needed to achieve microbial stability.

Bentonite and lysozyme should not be used concurrently because bentonite deactivates lysozyme. Bentonite is first left to completely settle out, followed by a careful racking, and then lysozyme is added to inhibit bacteria. Before bottling, a protein stability test is performed to ensure that the lysozyme will not cause any stability problems. If the stability test is positive, another bentonite fining is required until the wine is protein stable. See page 111 to learn more about protein stability in wine.

~

What is *double-salt precipitation* and how is it relevant to winemaking?

DOUBLE-SALT PRECIPITATION is a technique for reducing acidity in high-acid wine.

In winemaking, it is often desirable and at times required to reduce acidity in juice or wine for better balance. High acidity is a common problem in cool-climate grape-growing regions or where the growing season may have been marked by cool weather. And certain cultivars inherently have high acidity. Various vinification techniques, some of which make use of a deacidifying agent, are used for reducing acidity; for example, potassium bicarbonate is used for reducing tartaric acid by precipitating it in potassium bitartrate salt form.

These techniques work very well on reducing tartaric acid, the major acid found in grape juice and wine. But often, the problem is low tartaric acid compared to high malic acid content because of a poor vintage where grapes did not fully ripen or as found in cool-climate grapes. And malolactic fermentation to reduce the malic content may not be desirable because it is known to produce unsatisfactory organoleptic results—Riesling is one such wine. But some tartaric acid reduction may also be desired, for example, to prepare the wine for cold stabilization. The solution: *double-salt precipitation*—so called because it precipitates a double salt, as opposed to a simple salt like potassium tartrate. Specifically, it is a technique used for reducing tartaric and malic acids in approximately equal parts by precipitating them in their double-salt form using a special formulation consisting mainly of calcium carbonate (chalk) and a small percentage of calcium tartrate malate as a seeding aid.

Here, too, there is some very interesting acid chemistry that explains why double-salt precipitation is preferred over simply using calcium carbonate.

Wine has a pH usually in the range 3.10–3.50 and therefore, tartaric acid which has a first dissociation value in this range will dissociate into its bitartrate and tartrate ions. When calcium carbonate is added, it neutralizes tartaric acid only and precipitates calcium tartrate salt, however, this can take months to happen and creates instability issues but more importantly, calcium malate precipitates also form and impart an unappealing earthy taste.

Double-salt precipitation products, however, raise the pH of a calculated and measured part-volume of juice or wine pH to 4.5 which is within the range of the second dissociation values of tartaric and malic acid and easily precipitates the low-solubility double salt calcium tartrate malate in as less as thirty minutes. The part-volume of wine is then filtered and added back to the rest of the untreated wine to reduce total acidity as calculated. No tartrate instabilities, no unappealing taste—only clever chemistry.

∼

What is *delestage*—some kind of winemaker's dance?

No. DELESTAGE IS A RED winemaking technique.

Often, rich, full-bodied wines can be overly astringent in their youth, particularly those that have spent some time in oak barrels and may not be approachable before a few years of aging to tame the tannins. A technique called *delestage fermentation* can be used to make full-bodied wines more approachable when young and that exhibit a fruitier nose with a rounder, less astringent mouthfeel.

Delestage (from the French *délestage* meaning "lightening" in reference to the separation of wine and grape solids) is a fermentation–maceration technique used in red winemaking from grapes which gently extracts phenolic compounds by oxygenating the wine to produce a softer, less astringent wine exhibiting more fruit character. In fact, Dr. Bruce Zoecklein's research at Virginia Tech has demonstrated that delestage-fermented wines have a lower concentration of tannins and a higher concentration of esters—key compounds that contribute fruitiness to wine.

Delestage then is a two-step "rack-and-return" process whereby fermenting red wine is separated from the grape solids by racking and then returned to the fermenting vat or tank to re-soak the solids and then repeated daily.

Racking the fermenting wine oxygenates the wine and softens the astringent tannins through oxidation and also stabilizes its color. Racking during maceration and fermentation is the underlying difference from traditional maceration–fermentation where the juice ferments under a layer of carbon dioxide gas and is seldom aerated until racked at the end of fermentation. Pump-over (the recirculation of wine from the bottom of the fermentation vat to the top to soak the grape solids) is sometimes used for aerating the wine but does not provide the same effects as delestage because the wine is never separated entirely from the grape solids.

During delestage racking, the cap slowly falls to the bottom of the vat while the wine is allowed to drain completely under the weight of the grape solids. While the wine drains from the bottom valve of the vat or tank and into the receiving vat, a portion of harsh-tannin-imparting grape seeds are expelled and removed.

Following racking, the grape solids are allowed to settle separately from the fermenting wine for one or two hours or more depending on the size of the fermenting vat. The fermenting wine is returned to the vat over the cap using a gentle, high-volume pump to completely soak the grape solids for maximum color and flavor extraction.

This process is repeated daily until the end of fermentation. As fermentation progresses, more seeds are released from the grapes, and again, as many seeds as possible are removed during each racking operation.

An advantage of delestage is that the rack-and-return operation favors wine extraction from grape solids and increases free-run yield and therefore requires less pressing of the solids at the end of fermentation. Macerating enzymes can also be used to help break down cell walls of red grapes for a more gentle extraction of phenolic compounds thereby increasing the effects of delestage. Macerating enzymes are added to the must at crushing, i.e., before the start of fermentation, otherwise they will be inhibited by the presence of alcohol.

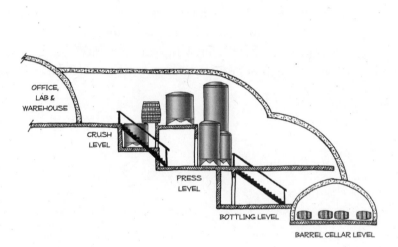

Example of an implementation of gravity-flow winemaking.
Courtesy of Malivoire Wine Company.

What is the big deal about gravity-flow winemaking?

GRAVITY-FLOW WINEMAKING refers to the flow of grapes, juice, and wine strictly under the action of gravity during winemaking, foregoing the use of electromechanical equipment, such as pumps and filters. Processing using such equipment is believed—though there is much debate about the effects—to adversely affect the quality as it overly processes wine which "whips" key aromas and flavor compounds and hastens oxidation.

In gravity-flow winemaking, grapes are first crushed at the winery's highest level and the crushed or pressed grapes, or juice, are transferred to fermentation tanks below at the next level. When fermentation is complete and the wine is to be racked into holding tanks or barrels, this too is done by gravity to the next level down. Bottling is done by gravity following multiple rackings and no filtration—gravity-flow proponents eschew the use of filters.

Wine Styles

≈

I AM REMINDED OF THE HILARIOUS quote from a fictitious scene unfolding in a restaurant and the patron asking for the wine list: "*Monsieur!* We have red wine and we have white wine," replied the waiter.

To those not partial to wine, some might wish it would be that simple—red or white. But life is not simple nor is it uninteresting, and wine would be just a boring, inconsequential beverage if it were not for its complexity and the plethora of styles. Wine is much more than just a drink or even a drink to complement food.

Wine is a mystical elixir that fosters friendship—or what Jonathan Nossiter (director of the film *Mondovino*) describes in *Liquid Memory* as "a vector of exchange between human beings," and conviviality, good health, and joie de vivre, unmatched by any other food or beverage. Every bottle has a story, whether it is about the vineyard, the vintage, the winery's or winemaker's reputation or label or perhaps even a special purchase from that memorable vacation in wine country. It is also the most adaptable beverage. It can be drunk on its own as an aperitif or for a fireside tête-à-tête, with food, with or as dessert, to celebrate a special occasion or to enjoy with a fine cigar or chocolate. There is a plethora of kinds and styles to suit any occasion or palate—from dry whites and full-bodied reds to rosés and off-dry or medium-sweet whites, sparkling wine, Icewine, Port, Sherry, oaked, unoaked, and organic wines. Technical know-how and technology aside, styles are only limited by the winemaker's creativity. But creativity requires setting aside those biases rooted in tradition.

In this section we answer questions often asked about the different kinds and styles of wines, the differences between wines in the same category, such as Port, and how these are produced. In the section *Wine Service*, we will look at why certain wines are best enjoyed with certain kinds of food.

Some Chardonnays are described as having buttery-like aromas and flavors while others do not.
Are all Chardonnays not alike?

NOT QUITE. ACTUALLY, THERE can be huge differences depending on the winemaker's desired style.

Chardonnay is—or was, according to those who have tired of this varietal and now ask for ABC, i.e., Anything But Chardonnay—without a doubt the most popular white wine, perhaps because of its universality or because it can be made into a wide array of styles to please any palate. If you are partial to a refreshing, fruity style, you may opt for an unoaked Chardonnay—that is, the wine has not been aged in oak barrels. If you prefer a full-bodied style with lots of oak, there are plenty of Chardonnays to choose from. Then there is a wide array of styles in between, all of which can be created using a combination of any of various winemaking techniques including barrel fermentation and aging, malolactic fermentation and lees stirring.

Barrel fermentation and aging are different, not only in the timing but also in the chemistry. The key difference is in the rate of extraction between oak aromas and flavors, and tannins. Tannins are extracted from oak wood at a faster rate and, as the wine ferments in barrels, yeast cells form complexes with the tannins and then precipitate; the net effect is reduced tannins and a softer wine. Barrel fermentation lasts weeks whereas barrel aging lasts months or even years.

When the wine has completed the alcoholic fermentation, it then goes through malolactic fermentation which produces diacetyl, or 2,3-butanedione, a diketone that imparts buttery and nutty aromas and flavors. It is the same chemical added to popcorn for taste.

The wine then undergoes barrel aging for several months or a year or more, during which time oak aromas and flavors still get extracted and lees or the sediment that forms at the bottom of barrels and which contain dead yeast cells are stirred to return them into suspension; this gives the wine that familiar yeasty or bread-like aroma. During barrel aging, wine also undergoes micro-oxygenation which further softens tannins while allowing delicate, subtle aromas and flavors to develop and evolve gracefully.

If all these techniques are practiced on Chardonnay, the result is a full-bodied, "oaky" wine with silky smooth tannins. Newer toasted barrels are used to add notes of toasted oak. Note that because a lot of tannins have been precipitated, barrel-fermented Chardonnay would still need aging to acquire more tannin to be able to age like a premium Chablis.

To create a light, fruity and unoaked Chardonnay, winemakers simply forego the above techniques. To create anything in between, winemakers may perform one or more of the techniques, most likely in large tanks and by adding oak chips, for example, to give the wine a tad more character without the use of barrels, lees can be stirred in the tank; or to give it some "smoothness," the wine can go through malolactic fermentation in tanks.

∾

What about Pinot Gris and Pinot Grigio, Syrah and Shiraz?

Pinot Gris and *Pinot Grigio* are names for the same grape variety, a mutation of Pinot Noir; the same is true for *Syrah* and *Shiraz*. The different names are used in different winemaking regions to denote the region's wine style.

Pinot Gris refers to the fuller-bodied and more complex style of wine from this grape variety produced in the Alsace region in northeastern France. Many are made in an off-dry or lightly sweet style; however, the best Alsatian Pinot Gris, produced from old, low-yielding vines, have an almost imperceptible high residual sugar content that is superbly well balanced with the acidity giving the wine long aging potential. The grapes are ideally grown over a long

Lees being stirred in a barrel of Chardonnay wine.

Frozen Vidal grapes on the vine ready for harvesting to make Icewine.

and cool summer. But it is Pinot Grigio, the style produced in northeastern Italy, more specifically in Friuli, Veneto and to a lesser extent, Trentino-Alto Adige, which has grown in popularity as a replacement for the ever-popular (unoaked) Chardonnay. Pinot Grigio emphasizes fruitiness and freshness, and so, it is typically characterized by high acidity and meant to be drunk young and is produced from higher-yield vines. It is not uncommon to see a light pinkish tint in Pinot Gris/Grigio; this is because the grapes have a pinkish or light purple skin, and so a small amount of color is transferred to the juice during pressing.

Syrah and Shiraz are used to make some of the most superlative red wines of the world, and which have become very fashionable, especially with those looking for alternatives to the more popular Cabernet Sauvignon, Cabernet Franc and Merlot-based wines. The grape variety is most well-suited in warmer climates to produce those luscious, concentrated "fruit bombs." *Syrah* refers to the style produced in the northern Rhône region in southern France that includes such great appellations as Hermitage, Condrieu, and Côte Rôtie; whereas *Shiraz* refers to the bolder style produced in Australia where it is often blended with one or both of the Cabernet varietals.

~

What is all the fuss about Beaujolais Nouveau? And why did my wine retailer tell me that I should drink that bottle of *nouveau* wine within the next couple of weeks?

BEAUJOLAIS NOUVEAU is a very young, fruity, red wine from the Beaujolais region, south of Burgundy in France, and which is made available on the third Thursday of November. The wine is made from grapes harvested that same fall season and is meant to be drunk as soon as it is made available. It is not intended for aging; it will actually deteriorate fairly rapidly, usually well within a couple of months because it is lacking the tannins that give wine its structure and aging potential. It is most often red although white varietals are now available, particularly from other parts of the world that have jumped on the *nouveau*-wine bandwagon such as *vino novello* in Italy.

The tradition started as a way to celebrate the end of the harvest but probably more so to sell some wine and generate much-needed cash flow in an already marginal business. It was certainly a clever marketing tactic—a small supply and a huge demand—popularized by the king of Beaujolais, Georges Duboeuf, with folks lining up for hours at wine shops to get their bottle of Beaujolais Nouveau. But the laws of economics reversed in the 1980s as wine consumers' palates became more sophisticated and wanting fuller-bodied wines with greater character and depth. The tradition continues, albeit, with much-reduced consumer interest.

So how can wine be ready in November when grapes are harvested in August or perhaps even September? The answer: carbonic maceration, a relatively new vinification technique developed by French enologist Michel Flanzy (1902–1992) in the late 1930s in the Languedoc-Roussillon region of southern France but popularized in Beaujolais.

Carbonic maceration is a vinification technique that triggers an intracellular fermentation within whole (uncrushed) berries to extract the maximum amount of fruit from grapes. As opposed to full-bodied red wines where the juice is allowed to macerate with the grape skins (intercellular fermentation) to extract maximum phenols, including color and tannins, in addition to the fruit, nouveau-style wines macerate for only a short period of time resulting in very little phenolic extraction. The result is a light-bodied wine with oodles of fruit and very little tannin but which must be drunk soon after production.

Grapes are placed in a pressure-resistant, stainless steel tank under a layer of carbon dioxide gas to create an anaerobic environment and to trigger an intracellular fermentation within berries which is enabled by grape enzymes, not yeast enzymes. During this intracellular fermentation, flavor compounds are extracted to give these wines their characteristic fresh fruit aromas but only a small amount of sugar gets converted to alcohol—up to approximately two percent. Intracellular fermentation in itself would therefore not be sufficient in making the final wine. Alcoholic fermentation is also required to run in parallel by allowing some juice from crushed grapes to interact with indigenous or cultured yeast to convert sugar into alcohol to obtain a wine with 11 to 12.5 percent alcohol. The juice is obtained by either crushing a small portion of the grape volume or by letting the weight of the grapes crush and split grapes at the bottom of the fermenting vat. As the juice at the bottom of the vat starts fermenting, it gives off carbon dioxide gas which displaces air and creates an anaerobic environment and provokes intracellular fermentation of whole berries above.

As alcoholic fermentation progresses, whole berries undergoing intracellular fermentation become softer and start bursting to release wine. To minimize phenolic extraction, free-run wine is separated only three or four days after the start of fermentation. Free-run wine is essentially wine obtained without any pressing. The must which will still contain whole but soft berries is then pressed to extract wine. This press-run wine is still rich in sugar content and is therefore added to the free-run wine, and alcoholic fermentation is then allowed to complete to dryness (the point at which, for all practical purposes, there is no more sugar to ferment). The wine is then fined and filtered to ensure it is crystal clear and that it remains stable once bottled.

Nouveau wines will have a lower total acidity than wines vinified by traditional winemaking. Less acidity is extracted during carbonic maceration and this in the presence of indigenous lactic acid bacteria. The reduced acidity creates a favorable environment for the lactic acid bacteria to convert the naturally occurring, sharper malic acid into the softer lactic acid by malolactic fermentation.

Although the exuberantly fruity Gamay grape is used in making red Beaujolais Nouveau, other grape varieties with low tannin content such as Pinot Noir, Carignan or even Concord can be used. Grape varieties such as Cabernet Sauvignon are inherently too tannic and would not be compatible with the light, fruity nouveau-style wines. White nouveau-style wines are also possible using fruity grape varieties having a high acid content, such as Sauvignon Blanc, for example. Low-acid varieties would result in a flat, dull wine with no zinging freshness.

~

Rot is rot, so why—and what—is *noble rot* a good thing?

NOBLE ROT SURE IS ROT but it is considered noble because it can turn grapes into a source of juice for making some of the most sought-after, age-worthy, delectably delicious sweet wines of the likes of fabled Château d'Yquem of Sauternes (Bordeaux) fame, Hungarian Tokaji Aszú or Eszencia, and German Trockenbeerenauslese (TBA) Prädikats. Very old vintages of Château d'Yquem from the late nineteenth century are still appearing at auctions.

Noble rot is gray mold, or more precisely, *Botrytis cinerea*, the anamorph of *Botryotinia fuckeliana* (I kid you not), a Jekyll-and-Hyde sort of mold—it can either spoil grape bunches or turn them into sugar-rich, nectar-producing fruit that can be made into hedonistic sweet wines.

Where weather is rainy or of high relative humidity, mold spores will cause grape berries to turn brown, but more importantly, it can start consuming precious sugar and cause berries to rot with the help of other microorganisms, a condition known as *sour-bunch rot*. Under perfect conditions of cool nights and warm days, *B. cinerea* mold spores can give rise to noble rot. If the day's temperature starts climbing along with winds after an early morning fog or dew, in this case the mold spores will dehydrate grape berries thereby increasing the concentration of sugar and acidity. Optimum conditions for noble rot growth require a temperature in the range 15°–20°C (59°–68°F) with a relative humidity greater than ninety percent.

Thin-skinned, tightly bunched grape varieties are most prone to *B. cinerea*, particularly where air circulation through the canopy is limited from, for example, excessive foliage. In Sauternes, Sauvignon Blanc and Sémillon are two varieties that can produce excellent brotytized wines in favorable vintages. In Hungary, where botrytized Eszencia and Aszú wines have been made since at least the 1630s, Furmint and Hárslevelű are the main varieties. The juice for making Eszencia is so sweet that fermentation struggles along for months or years to produce a mere two percent alcohol, though it is typically in the five-to-six percent range. Aszú is also the pride of Hungarians, so much so that it is sung in their national anthem—the *Himnusz*. So next time you drink a Tokaji Aszú, be sure to stand up and salute our Hungarian winemaking friends.

~

What is ice wine and how is it made?

ICE WINE IS AN IMPECCABLY well-balanced, high-acidity, sweet dessert wine with aromas of peach, apricot, litchi and nutty flavors and is produced from grapes naturally frozen on the vines. Ice wine originated in 1794 in Franconia, Germany where it is called *Eiswein*. As with many discoveries, it was the result of an accident. (This discovery "fact" is not well documented. Since it was best documented later in an 1830 "re-discovery," Dromersheim, Germany is said to be the rightful birthplace of *Eiswein*.) As with much of Europe plagued by cold weather, Germany suffered a cold growing season in 1794 and let their Riesling grapes hang on the vines a while longer in the hope that warmer temperatures would come to help grapes ripen. Instead, a nasty frost caused the grapes to freeze but a determined winemaker set out to harvest the grapes anyway. He was able to press the frozen grape berries and ferment the syrupy juice. How he managed the fermentation is not clear given our current knowledge of the challenges of making ice wine.

Donald Ziraldo and Karl Kaiser, who co-founded Inniskillin Wines in 1974 and pioneered ice wine in the Niagara Peninsula in Ontario, have aptly named this art as *extreme winemaking*. Their 1989 Vidal Icewine won the Grand Prix d'Honneur at the international Vinexpo event in Bordeaux in 1991.

And so it is that Canada—more specifically Ontario—has become world-renowned for its ice wine where it is trademarked and officially called *Icewine*. Unlike Germany where the winter season is not as predictable, Ontario is able to produce Icewine year after year.

Icewine production in Ontario is governed by the bylaws and standards of the Vintners Quality Alliance (VQA), which also governs all aspects of viticulture, winemaking and marketing of wines produced from locally grown grapes. For Icewine, VQA mandates that grapes be harvested at a minimum sugar concentration of thirty-five percent by weight and at no more than $-8°C$ ($18°F$), which means that harvesting really must occur at $-10°C$ ($14°F$) or colder to allow for slight temperature increases by the time the grapes are handled when they arrive at the winery. If these conditions are not met, the wine cannot be labeled as Icewine. To maintain the cold temperature of grapes, small wineries harvest by hand in the middle of the night. Large wineries equipped with machinery and equipment to process grapes rapidly may harvest during the day.

The simple explanation of letting grapes freeze on the vines is that the cold temperature causes the water content in grape berries to freeze and therefore concentrate sugars, acids and flavor compounds. But it gets much more interesting once we take a closer look at the biochemistry of grape berry cells during the freezing process.

As berries start freezing—which happens from the outside of the berries towards the center—there is an imbalance in osmotic pressure between water outside and inside berries. The greater external pressure causes water from inside berries to flow through cell walls and out the grape skins, causing partial dehydration, which in turn hastens freezing inside berries and further concentrating those delicious flavors, sugars and acids.

Whole-cluster grapes are pressed outdoors immediately following harvesting at subfreezing temperatures to extract the sugar-rich syrup from the marble-hard berries and to discard the frozen water content. The syrup is allowed to warm up before being inoculated for fermentation—a process that takes considerably longer than fermentation in dry wines, often up to three months or more depending on sugar content in the juice. The wine is then sterile filtered to remove any active yeast still present after fermentation has stopped, and is then aged a minimum of six months before it is bottled and commercialized.

Fermentation will stop at around eleven percent alcohol and yield a very sweet wine with superb acidity, intense flavors and sublime complexity. The high price of Icewine is due to high viticulture management costs but more importantly, due to the low grape yields. Since more than seventy percent of grape juice is actually water, significant juice volume is lost when pressing frozen grapes.

As a significant amount of tartaric acid would have precipitated as potassium bitartrate while grapes were freezing on the vines, total acidity (TA) in Icewine juice comprises a high percentage of malic acid, in the order of 65–75 percent and varies with the pH of the juice. During fermentation, malic acid concentration decreases but total acidity increases due to acetic acid production resulting from yeast fermenting under stressful conditions and due to succinic acid production from yeast fermentation. Acetic acid, which will be relatively higher than in other types of wines, contributes to higher volatile acidity (VA) and is actually beneficial at low levels in Icewine by contributing to aroma and flavor development. Succinic acid enhances flavors by contributing a salty and bitter taste.

The most common grape variety for making white Icewine is Vidal, a hybrid of *V. vinifera* and *V. riparia* species, as it can weather the harsh, cold climate better owing to its thick skin. Riesling and Gewürztraminer Icewines are also highly sought after as these *V. vinifera* varieties are more nuanced resulting in much more complex aromas and flavors. There are now red Icewines made from such varieties as Cabernet Franc and Merlot.

Making ice wine is a lot of work and very risky. Where weather conditions do not allow for the natural freezing of grapes on the vines or if the grapes cannot attain optimum sugar and acidity levels, grapes can be artificially frozen in temperature-controlled containers before vinification. This controversial process, called *cryoextraction*, is commonly practiced nowadays by reputable wineries in sweet-wine production although certain countries, such as Canada and Germany, do not allow such wines to be labeled Icewine or Eiswein. A common name found on commercially produced ice wine-style wine by cryoextraction is *vin de glace*. Cryoextraction consists of freezing the grape juice in a deep freezer to extract the sugar-rich syrup and leave the water content behind. The syrup is then fermented and processed as regular ice wine.

Try Icewine with your favorite dessert or simply on its own after dinner—it does not get any better.

∽

What is the difference between Port and Sherry wines?

Port is a fortified, sweet, red wine from the Oporto region in Portugal's Douro Valley, although there are port-style wines from other regions. In true Port production, no sugar is added. Instead, while the wine is still fermenting, a distilled spirit such as brandy produced from grapes from the same region, is added to stop the fermentation—the sudden addition of high alcohol will inhibit any yeast activity—and the wine retains natural sugar and high alcohol, typically around twenty percent. The wine is then aged in oak barrels to add further aroma and flavor complexities. There are many Port wine styles depending on maturation (aging) and methods for imparting oak aromas and flavors, and include ruby, tawny, vintage, and late-bottled vintage (LBV) Ports, and now, even pink Port which is meant to be drunk cold as an aperitif. Vintage Port, the bellwether of Ports, is produced from a blend of the best wines from the best grapes from multiple vineyards from a single vintage, is aged only two years in oak barrels and is then bottled, unfiltered, where it can be aged for ten, twenty, thirty or more years. By comparison, late-bottled vintage (LBV) Port is produced from declassified vintage Port (Port not deemed to have the required quality of vintage Port) and bottled after four to six years following the harvest. It is usually filtered and, therefore, does not throw heavy sediment like vintage Port.

Sherry is a fortified white wine from Spain's Jerez de la Frontera region, although again, other regions produce sherry-style wines ranging in style from dry to sweet. Similar to Port production, brandy is added to fortify the wine, however, the wine is left to ferment to dryness before fortification. Fino Sherry is the driest and by using various winemaking techniques, different styles and levels of sweetness can be created, such as manzanilla, amontillado, oloroso and cream sherry. An interesting technique in Sherry-making is the use of flor yeast or surface yeast which forms on the surface of wine in partially filled casks or barrels. The wine is aged under the thick layer of yeast to let it develop its familiar nutty, "bready" and yeasty aromas. Another technique is the *solera* process where wine is aged in barrels, and with each new vintage, some wine from older vintages is blended into barrels of the newer vintage. The process is repeated year over year; the result is a wine that can contain wine from as much as a hundred years ago, albeit, a very small amount, but which develops layers and layers of complex aromas and flavors.

~

How is Champagne made and why is it so expensive?

SPARKLING WINE, BUBBLY, or more correctly, *vin mousseux* for the purists, is the wine par excellence to raise a toast, to celebrate a special occasion, or to share a romantic moment in a hot tub (see page 178 for health concerns about this practice). The magic of sparkling wine, such as Champagne, always brings a festive mood to any occasion. But how little people realize how much work goes into producing a bottle of mousseux. There is some great chemistry and physics in every bottle, from the wine to the glass and cork. The combination of intensive, manual work and wine that needs several years of cellaring explains the high cost of sparkling wine. This process is for the most part automated today in the larger wineries.

Sparkling wine is produced from still wine known as the *cuvée* in Champagne and is usually an *assemblage* or "blend" of the best wines. It involves conducting a second alcoholic fermentation by one of two methods to produce the carbon dioxide gas bubbles or by a variation of these.

The method used in true Champagne—sparkling wine that can only be called as such if produced in the Champagne region— involves conducting a second alcoholic fermentation in bottles that have to withstand up to 6 bars (90 psi) of pressure or more, which explains why the glass is twice as heavy as the glass of a still-wine bottle. About 24 grams of sugar (plus yeast, in what is known as the *liqueur de tirage*) is required for bottle fermentation, which adds 1.5% alcohol to the bubbly and traps the resulting carbon dioxide in the wine that produces the effervescence when the bottle is uncorked. Known as *prise de mousse* in French, this bottle-fermentation technique is the underlying principle of the *méthode champenoise* traditional process, often, though erroneously, credited to Dom Pierre Pérignon (ca. 1638–1715), the cellar master and monk at the Benedictine Abbaye d'Hautvillers, now of Moët & Chandon fame. In that era of winemaking, sugar could not be measured—at least not accurately enough to have a predictable outcome— hence why some argue that Dom Pérignon could not be credited with developing the exact technique.

The méthode champenoise is also used in the production of premium Californian and Italian sparkling wines as well as Spanish *cava*, where the method is usually referred to as *traditional method* (*méthode traditionelle*) or *classical method* (*méthode classique*).

In this method, the sparkling wine is kept in the same bottle throughout the second fermentation during the extended period of aging on the lees, a process known as *tirage*, when the yeast undergoes autolysis to give Champagne its distinctive and complex aromas and flavors. The yeast deposit (lees) from the long and cool fermentation is then collected in a special cap, the *bidule*, by inverting the bottle from a horizontal to a vertical position in systematic and progressive fashion—a process known as *riddling* or *remuage* in French—each day for twenty-one days. The neck of the bottle is then frozen to remove the cap and frozen deposit without disturbing the clarity of the wine. This bottle-clarification process is known as *dégorgement* or disgorgement. A sweet solution, the *liqueur d'expédition* or dosage, is then added to each bottle to sweeten the wine and balance the high acidity according to the winery's house style, namely: up to 6 g/L of residual sugar for an *Extra Brut* (also known as *Brut de Brut, Brut Nature, Bone Dry*) style; up to 15 g/L for *Brut*, 12–20 g/L for *Extra Dry* (*Extra Sec, Extra Trocken*); 17–35 g/L for *Dry* (*Sec, Trocken, Secco*); 35–50 g/L for *Off-Dry* (*Demi Sec, Doux, Semi-Dry, Halbtrocken, Abboccato, Medium Sweet*); and more than 50 g/L for *Sweet* (*Doux, Dolce*). [Terminology can be confusing as each wine-making region uses different definitions that use different ranges of residual sugar.] The dosage may contain older wine or a liqueur. Some believe that the secret in making premium-quality sparkling wine is in the dosage, and so the dosage formulation is often a well-kept secret. Lastly, a very-high-density, cylindrically shaped cork is inserted and kept in place by a muselet. The cork is mushroom-shaped when popped because the portion above the opening is dry while the bottom expanded as it has been in contact with the wine for an extended period of time.

It is clearly a laborious process that also requires a lot of experience to achieve a good quality sparkling wine which is judged on both the size and the amount of bubbles; endless, tiny, rapid-forming and long-lasting bubbles are a sure sign of an ultra-premium sparkling wine. Much of the process is now automated with equipment that reduces manual intervention to a bare minimum, including riddling, which is now performed by gyropalettes. Bottles are placed in the inverted position in these large bins and the riddling action is under the precise control of a robotized arm.

Another simpler method consists in conducting a bulk second fermentation in stainless steel, pressure-resistant tanks. This tank-fermentation method, known as the *cuve close* or *Charmat process*, bypasses the need for bottle fermentation, riddling and disgorgement. The sparkling wine is then refrigerated for bottling under pressure to minimize gas loss. This process is less costly compared to the méthode champenoise, and is commonly used in commercial winemaking in such wines as Asti Spumante, the popular low-alcohol, sweet sparkling wine from Piedmont, Italy.

Another little-known fact is that white sparkling wine can be produced from white or red grape varieties, or a combination of both as done in Champagne where Chardonnay, Pinot Noir and Pinot Meunier are used. In Burgundy, for example, they produce *blanc de blancs* (white from white grapes) bubbly from Chardonnay and *blanc de noirs* (white from "black" grapes) from Pinot Noir.

And why are some sparkling wines vintage-dated and not others?

Sparkling wine producers like to maintain a specific style of bubbly from year to year that consumers have come to rely on, and to achieve this, they blend cuvées from two or more vintages. These wines are labeled as NV (non-vintage) or designated as multi-vintage. If the quality of a vintage cuvée is outstanding, it is used for their premium vintage-dated sparkling wine which is also most often a blend of different cuvées but all from the same vintage.

Note that letting bubbly gush out uncontrollably when uncorking a bottle is poor etiquette and a sure way to upset the winemaker (when present). Now, if only I could enlighten those F1 podium-winners as to the hard work made by winemakers to get those bubbles in the wine!

~

Is there any other way to make sparkling wine at home?

YES. IN FACT, HOME WINEMAKERS have three simple and inexpensive alternatives to produce early-drinking, sparkling wines: using a sparkling wine kit, by carbonation or using dialysis tubing.

There are now easy-to-use kits with concentrate and all necessary ingredients for making sparkling wine. The kits use a variation of the traditional method; they still ferment in the bottle but the sediment is not disgorged. The finished wine requires careful pouring from the bottle when serving so as not to disturb the sediment at the bottom.

Carbonation is the process used in soft-drink production where a beverage is injected with carbon dioxide gas. This method produces very good sparkling wine with much less effort and risk but with fewer and larger bubbles that fade quickly compared to premium sparkling wines.

But one of the most exciting ways of making bubbly at home is by dialysis. The dialysis-tubing method is an ingenious way of making traditional-method sparkling wine without the need to riddle and disgorge. It is an amazingly simple alternative that produces excellent results. The method involves packaging yeast in dialysis tubing or membrane which is made of a semi-permeable polymer, such as regenerated cellulose, and will initiate bottle fermentation, unlike the traditional method where a sugar–yeast solution is pitched directly into the base wine. Dialysis is a simple process, known as

Traditionally, Port wine was shipped in barrels via the Douro River in Portugal.

Vintage sparkling wine on riddling racks aging deep in the cellars of Schramsberg Vineyards in Calistoga, CA.

osmosis, in which small solutes (sugar) diffuse from a high concentration solution (wine) to a low concentration solution (yeast culture) across a semi-permeable membrane until equilibrium is reached. The yeast in the tubing is allowed to interact with the sugar in the wine through the membrane but the larger-sized spent lees from fermentation remain trapped in the tubing therefore making "disgorging" a trivial operation. Once bottle fermentation is complete, the dialysis tubing with the spent yeast is simply removed, and *voilà*, a clear sparkling wine.

How clever! It is not a traditional method of sparkling winemaking but your friends and family might well mistake your bubbly with premium commercial sparkling wine. Let's raise a toast to dialyzed bubbly.

~

Speaking of bubbly—do you know how many bubbles there are in a bottle of sparkling wine?

WHAT AN INTERESTING QUESTION!

Sparkling wine is without a doubt my favorite wine; it makes for a superb *apéro* or a great accompaniment to crustaceans. But for a lack of time or curiosity, I never did ask myself this question. Perhaps I have been too busy enjoying my bubbly. But scientist Bill Lembeck was curious enough to take the time to figure this one out. This would surely be a challenge, even for the most well-versed chemistry scholar. Given the wide array of sparkling wine styles, the best we can expect is an estimation based on a typical 750-mL bottle of, say, Champagne—the standard to which all bubblies are measured. Lembeck figured that if he can determine the amount of carbon dioxide dissolved in a bottle of bubbly, he can estimate the number of bubbles. But first, let's look at the physical chemistry of how bubbles are created when the cork is pulled.

Carbon dioxide gas exists in dissolved form in sparkling wine, and the pressure exerted in the closed bottle causes the gas to remain dissolved. However, according to Henry's Law, as soon as the cork is pulled, the higher gas pressure in the wine will slowly work towards equilibrium with the atmospheric pressure just above the surface of the wine. (This is the same phenomenon as when opening a can of soft drink—after several days and depending on temperature, the drink goes flat. Henry's Law more specifically states that, at a constant temperature, the volume of gas dissolved in a given volume of liquid is directly proportional to the partial pressure of that gas in equilibrium with that liquid.) As the gas and atmospheric pressures slowly move towards thermodynamic equilibrium, carbon dioxide gas becomes less soluble and causes *bubble nucleation* or the formation of microbubbles in nucleation sites. Any imperfections in the glass, such as scratches or residues, as well as microscopic colloids still in suspension in the wine will hasten bubble nucleation and give rise to continuous streams of rapidly forming tiny bubbles dancing endlessly to the surface of the wine. Bubbles then burst into tiny droplets to release all those delightful aromas. That is the reason why sparkling wine flutes washed with detergents tend to show fewer bubbling activity—the detergent will "seal" glass imperfections and reduce the surface area of nucleation sites.

Here are Lembeck's calculations according to the website beekmanwine.com.

At average room temperature, Champagne is under approximately 6 bars (90 psi) of pressure which is about three times the amount of pressure in car tires—so now you know why sparkling wine bottles can be explosive. Lembeck used 5.5 bars at 20°C (68°F) in his calculations; that corresponds to 4,125 milliliters (mL) of carbon dioxide gas in a *closed* 750-mL bottle.

Now comes the tricky part—bubble size. The best sparkling wines have the tiniest bubbles (to understand this, compare bubble sizes in a glass of Champagne and a glass of carbonated soft drink). With the use of an optical comparator—a device that measures the

size of objects using a magnified silhouette projected on a screen—
he determined that the average bubble measures 0.5 mm in diameter,
which computes into a volume of 69 millionth of one mL. Applying
Henry's Law, there is then at least 750 mL of dissolved carbon dioxide
that would remain trapped in the bottle and which must be
subtracted from the total in the bottle. The volume of carbon dioxide
gas is then 3,375 mL, and therefore, 3,375 mL divided by 69 millionths of one mL gives roughly 49 million bubbles in a bottle of
Champagne. *And voilà!*

But my money would be on Champagne expert Gérard Liger-
Belair, Associate Professor of Physical Sciences at the University of
Reims Champagne-Ardenne, whose starting assumption in *Uncorked: The Science of Champagne* estimates that there is approximately 700 mL of gaseous carbon dioxide in a flute of Champagne
(or 5,250 mL in a bottle). He then calculated that a flute of the bubbly
contains about 11 million bubbles or more than 80 million bubbles
in a standard bottle.

That many bubbles would give new meaning to "bubble bath"
and Marilyn Monroe did just that. She is reported to have taken a
long, luxurious bubble bath in a tub filled with Champagne—yep,
all of 350 bottles!

The number of bubbles in Champagne would not be serious
business unless some "real" research—the type that has serious
money to back it up—would be undertaken to measure the size of
bubbles. Well, the prestigious Champagne house of Moët & Chandon
of Dom Pérignon fame and who has been making Champagne since
1743, partnered with beer-making giant Heineken in the late 1980s
to do just that and threw $7 million at it. Ok, their goal, according
to website beekmanwine.com was mainly to…

> understand and study the influence of chemical and
> physical parameters on the formation of bubbles and the
> stability of the mousse … At the heart of this research was
> a camera-based, computer-linked 'artificial vision' system

built by ITMI (*Industrie et Technolgie de la Machine*), which actually recorded the release of bubbles and counted them. According to [head of research] Monsieur Dutertre, there are on average 250 million bubbles in a bottle (of Champagne, not lager!).

Now that is quite a significant difference in the estimated number of bubbles. Did Lembeck and Liger-Belair use some cheap knockoff sparkling or carbonated bubbly while Moët & Chandon–Heineken used high-end Champagne? This is enough to make my head spin and I have not had any Champagne yet.

∼

What is *moonshine*? Is grappa moonshine? How is it made?

MOONSHINE IS DEFINED as distilled corn whiskey but it is commonly used to refer to any type of liquor, including grappa, obtained by distillation.

Grappa contains 38–43 percent alcohol and is made from *vinaccia*—the pomace or the remnants of pressed fermented grape skins—as in the authentic method. It can also be made from wine, in which case it is called *brandy*, but all too often it is wine considered faulty and no longer marketable—the result is a poorer-quality distillate.

Grappa has resurged as a popular digestif and the many offerings of the moonshine in designer bottles is proof of the booming popularity. It is no small business; like Cognac and other popular distilled spirits or wines (Champagne, Icewine, etc.), the word "grappa" is protected under Italian and EU laws.

Distillation is the process of separating two liquids by virtue of their difference in boiling points. In the case of wine distillation, the two liquids are water (yes, wine consists of roughly eighty-five percent water), and pure water boils at 100°C (212°F), and ethyl alcohol which boils at 78.3°C (173°F) in its pure form. The boiling point of wine is, therefore, in that temperature range and will be affected by other wine constituents, such as sugars, other alcohols, phenols, and many, many volatile components; a typical wine with thirteen percent alcohol can be expected to have a boiling point around 91°C (196°F).

To make grappa, wine is heated to its boiling point in an *alambicco* to vaporize the ethyl alcohol, and then channeling the alcohol steam through a condenser that cools it down and condenses it back into liquid alcohol—the distillate. However, wine also contains small amounts of other low-boiling-point compounds, many of which are undesirable, such as methyl alcohol which has a boiling point of 64.5°C (148°F). Methyl alcohol will therefore vaporize before ethyl alcohol and it will be part of the first fraction of the distillate in what is known as the *head*. The small amount of methyl alcohol in wine is of no concern, however, it has toxic effects (causing blindness) now that it is present in higher concentration in the head and so it is discarded or sent to other processors to turn into other products. As the distillation process progresses, purer ethyl alcohol is collected in the second fraction, and towards the tail end, those compounds less volatile than ethyl alcohol, such as higher alcohols (e.g., isoamyl and isobutyl) also known as *fusel oils* will become part of the third fraction or the *tail* of the distillate. The tail too is undesirable which can be tricky to separate in simple distillation techniques, such as still (laboratory scale) distillation.

Fractional distillation is used to circumvent these problems and to recover the purest portion of ethyl alcohol, leaving the head and tail behind. Fractional distillation is also used to recover those highly volatile aromatic compounds which are returned to the distillate to give grappa its spectrum of aromas.

Note that home distillation is illegal in Canada and the U.S. because making it is dangerous—we have all heard of horror stories of houses going up in smoke with a big bang—and the stuff really can make you blind if you do not know your chemistry.

Now, I am still trying to find a way to explain to my dad the wine stains on my room's ceiling, the result of a young chemist trying some after-school experiment. I forgot the boiling chips (to control the boiling). I think I will go have a glass of grappa to muster courage before I go visit my dad and come clean.

~

Wine Faults

~

YOUR GUESTS ARE COMFORTABLY seated at the dinner table waiting to be delighted by your culinary talents but mainly by your wine selection. After all, you have been praising and hyping *that* special bottle of wine—the one you proudly made or brought back from your last trip to Tuscany—waiting for the right occasion to be opened. With all eyes on the bottle, you engage into a soliloquy of superlatives to build up more suspense as you carefully remove the foil and uncork the bottle with that music-to-the-ear pop. Everything is perfect. You pour yourself a splash into a big goblet. You take a quick sniff. The look on your face quickly changes from cheerful to troubled and your guests can sense something is wrong. You take a sip, swoosh it in your mouth, but the taste confirms your worst fears. The wine is "corked." It smells musty, sort of like wet newspaper, and it is devoid of those promised fruity aromas. What a disappointment! How to explain this to your guests?

This is not an uncommon occurrence quite unfortunately. So often, especially when expectations are set high, a bottle of disappointingly flawed wine can send you in a frenzy searching for causes at the root of the problem. Whether the wine is corked, oxidized, smells of barnyard, or perhaps of rotten eggs, you are suddenly at a loss trying to understand what happened, even more so if *you* are the winemaker. It is a wine aficionado's or winemaker's worst nightmare.

Given wine's complex chemistry, biochemistry, and micro-biology, it is highly prone to a range of instabilities that can suddenly or serendipitously translate into faults or spoilage. The winemaker's duty is to process wine to avoid such faults or spoilage that could occur under normal conditions but the bigger challenge is protecting wine that is subjected to abnormal conditions, such as stored in a refrigerator for an extended period of time or, quite the opposite, the bottle is stored in the trunk of a car on a hot summer day.

In this section, we will examine some of the more common wine faults and try to understand where they originate. This should help you assess whether or not to return with confidence a faulty bottle to the sommelier when dining in a fine establishment.

∾

I understand the concept of oxidation in wines and I can recognize an oxidized wine but what is meant by "a wine is reduced"? I am sure it has nothing to do with how much wine is left in the bottle.

Most wine drinkers can recognize an oxidized wine—it takes on nutty-like aromas and the color shows brown hues in reds and golden hues in whites but it seems that only experienced wine tasters can detect—or know about—reduction. Let's examine the underlying chemistry to see what is happening.

Oxidation is a chemical reaction where a substance loses electrons or which may acquire oxygen or lose hydrogen atoms. Reduction is the inverse—that is, a chemical reaction where a substance gains electrons or which may lose oxygen or gain hydrogen atoms. To the chemist, oxidation and reduction are more precisely an increase and decrease in oxidation number, respectively, but we will use the former definition for simplicity. An oxidizing agent is known

97

as an *oxidant* whereas a reducing agent is most often referred to as an *antioxidant.*

Oxidation and reduction are paired reactions or a *redox pair* because chemical reactions are balanced. For example, when one substance gains oxygen atoms, another substance loses the oxygen atoms. The potential of compounds to oxidize or reduce is measured by what is known as *redox potential* and it is relatively higher in reds than in whites as white wines are more protected from air during winemaking. Now, let's see what happens when we bring sulfur into the equation.

First, as we know, oxygen is an oxidant and wine's number one enemy because it causes key compounds to oxidize—and so it would itself be reduced—with ethanol molecules losing a hydrogen atom resulting in an increase in the number of carbon–oxygen bonds to form acetaldehyde which imparts the familiar nut-like smell associated with oxidation. If oxidation is allowed to continue, then acetic acid sets in if acetic acid bacteria are present and causes the wine to spoil. By adding sulfite, sulfur dioxide is released which then scavenges oxygen and protects the wine from oxidation. However, if there is a high concentration of sulfur—from vineyard sulfur-based sprays as well as other sulfur-containing components such as amino acids—sulfur starts interacting with other wine components. These interactions may give rise to foul-smelling, sulfur-based compounds known as *thiols* (mercaptans) which are characterized by sulfhydryl (–SH) groups and which impart a disagreeable odor of onions and garlic. At low levels, these compounds may go undetected, however, the wine becomes muted and hides any fruity character it may have—and is said to be reduced.

Reduction is more common in reds where the high concentration of tannins reacts with oxygen, thus rendering the wine reductive. But we should not confuse reduction—the absence of a fruity character—with a detectable smell of sulfur dioxide which is indicative of over-sulfiting and definitely a fault. Reduction is not a fault.

The best example of oxidation and reduction, however, is the temporary, albeit, alarmingly looking browning in white wines, as in the famous case of Napa Valley's Chateau Montelena's 1973 Chardonnay. The case was also seen in *Bottle Shock*, a movie loosely based on the historic 1976 Judgment of Paris that launched the California wine industry to international prominence when Napa wines rated higher than their French counterparts in a blind tasting.

Montelena's Chardonnay tasted as beautifully as the winemaker intended it to taste; but unfortunately, the wine had suddenly turned a copper color in what looked like oxidation. Jim Barrett, the dejected owner, was looking to dispose of the "oxidized" wine until a University of California at Davis (a renowned enology university) professor explained that white wine contains a browning enzyme that causes a temporary change in color in wines that are produced in the *total* absence of air. As white wine is highly susceptible to oxidation, winemakers try to minimize exposure of the wine to air, and the little oxygen that the wine receives causes those enzymes to catalyze oxidation and the browning compounds to become colorless.

Specifically, the browning enzyme polyphenol oxidase causes caftaric acid and diphenols in white wine to oxidize when exposed to air. The oxidized compounds then react with glutathione, a tripeptide (a polymer formed by combining three alpha-amino acids) with strong antioxidant properties to form colorless glutathione–hydroxycinnamic acid complexes that do not react further. However, in the total absence of oxygen, the polyphenol oxidase enzymes are inactivated and cause the acid complexes to turn a copper color and then slowly back to colorless when the enzymes catalyze oxidation in the bottle.

And yes, Chateau Montelena's 1973 Chardonnay placed first in a tasting of ten Chardonnays, some of which included highly respected Burgundies. Bottles of the prized wine are now on display at the Smithsonian National Museum of American History in Washington, D.C. Reds? Top honors went to Stag's Leap Wine Cellars'

1973 wine, ahead of such wines as the 1970 vintage from Château Mouton Rothschild, Château Montrose and Château Haut-Brion. "*Scandalous!*" the French reacted. That forever changed the image of Californian wines.

∾

I brought back a great bottle of wine that I tasted at a vineyard I visited in Burgundy. I opened the bottle a few days later but the wine did not quite taste the same as I remember; it seemed to have lost its fruitiness. What could have happened?

BOTTLE SHOCK—THE PHYSICAL phenomenon, not the movie by the same name—is the likely culprit, though wine drunk at home often tastes "different" than when sampled in a romantic setting in the seductive vineyards of the world.

Bottle shock is about wine stress that results from excessive handling or vibrations from, for example, a long journey in a car. It is different from bottle sickness, and, though used interchangeably with "bottle shock," the two phenomena are different.

Bottle sickness refers to a wine with muted aromas and flavors, seemingly devoid of the fruity aromas, believed to be the result of rapid oxidation during the bottling process which causes a small amount of acetaldehyde to form. Once the bottle is corked, the condition slowly disappears over the course of the next month or so as acetaldehyde reacts with sulfur dioxide and phenols and the fruity aromas come out again.

So if you want to reminisce about that great, romantic wine tour in some faraway country, best to lay down that special bottle for a couple of months. It will *never* taste exactly the same but it will be very close ... if you close your eyes and concentrate on those memories.

∾

What is all the hoopla about in the ongoing debate between natural corks and screwcaps?

THREE LETTERS: T, C, A. Wretched TCA!

TCA, or 2,4,6-trichloroanisole, is a compound that produces a moldy, musty smell and is the result of a chemical reaction between phenolic compounds present in both oak wood (*Q. suber*) and wines and mold or chlorine, and which can be detected at extremely low concentrations in the ng/L, or parts per trillion (ppt), range. A wine affected by TCA is termed *corked* or what the French call *bouchonné*. Although TCA poses no health hazards, it is a serious wine fault as the wine becomes devoid of its complex flavors and aromas that we seek out so much. Some wineries claim that as much as twenty percent of wine is spoiled by TCA although five to ten percent is a more realistic range. In the worst case, TCA can propagate to contaminate an entire cellar or winery making it almost impossible to eradicate, and some wineries, such as historic Hanzell Vineyards in Sonoma, California have paid dearly to clean up contaminated cellars.

Wines (and wineries) are at risk if using poorly processed natural corks or corks containing some percentage of natural raw material, such as agglomerates or hybrid corks or if using chlorine around the wine cellar.

Natural corks are produced from the bark of oak trees which inherently have a high phenolic content. However, mold can grow on oak wood after the bark has been stripped from the tree and laid in piles in the cork groves. Once corks are punched out from the bark segments and processed at the facility, producers would in the past, eradicate molds and bacteria by bleaching and disinfecting corks with a chlorine solution. Although any chlorine residue was to be neutralized with oxalic acid, only a miniscule amount of chlorine, as little as one part per trillion (ppt), could cause TCA to form and adversely contaminate wine. This underlines the challenge of totally eradicating this foul-smelling compound, although many people can

Chateau Montelena's 1973 Chardonnay placed first at the
1976 Paris Tasting.

The Vino-Lok® glass closure. Could this be the closure
of the future?

only detect it at much higher levels, e.g., 10 ppt. As an illustrative example of the impact of TCA, Purdue University Associate Professor and Enologist Dr. Christian E. Butzke once estimated that one tablespoon of pure TCA could destroy all of the wine produced in the United States. Today, cork producers process and wash corks using hydrogen peroxide or to a lesser extent, potassium metabisulfite which have greatly reduced the risk of TCA taint.

Contamination in bottled wine is a result of the wine coming into contact with an infected cork while the bottle is stored on its side to keep the cork moist. If a bottle is stored upright, the cork could dry out and then contract and would no longer provide a good seal. Air would be allowed in and cause the wine to oxidize and eventually spoil.

Unfortunately, TCA contamination is not limited to corks produced from natural material. It can find its roots just about anywhere in the winery where the mold can grow, such as oak barrels, cardboard cases, or empty bottles or where chlorine vapor from chlorine-based cleaning agents may find its way on equipment or into barrels. This is cause for concern and can be disheartening to winemakers trying to zero in on the source of contamination. Detecting TCA contamination in the cellar is not easy, let alone trying to eradicate the problem.

So, is all the hoopla worth the investment to convert to screwcaps? Those who have paid dearly for TCA infection will not hesitate to say that it is all worth it. For the traditionalists, the data is perhaps not convincing—not just yet. But screwcaps are indeed gaining wide acceptance among consumers and wineries not inhibited by tradition. Many wineries have switched their entire production to screwcaps, including their premium wines. Screwcaps have proven to provide a perfect, inert seal, though some consumers are reporting detecting reductive notes (see page 97); but those disappear as the wine is poured into the glass.

Another important advantage of screwcaps is reduced bottle

variation—a well-known phenomenon with natural cork closures where wine in bottles from even the same case can taste and smell differently. That is because natural cork quality is not perfectly consistent by its very nature and, therefore, has different oxygen transfer rates (OTR)—that is, the rate at which oxygen penetrates through and around the cork. Screwcaps theoretically provide improved OTR consistency and, therefore, almost non-existent bottle variation.

If I had to choose an alternate closure "technology" for its long-term potential *and* consumer acceptance, I would probably bet on glass closures, such as the stylish Vino-Lok®. The Vino-Lok glass closure is the invention of the German division of Alcoa and was commercialized in 2004. German and Austrian wineries have embraced the new glass closure but it does not seem to have caught on yet in other winemaking regions. Vino-Lok is a closure manufactured entirely of glass and includes an O-ring to ensure an airtight seal with the bottle. A short aluminum capsule over the Vino-Lok completes the packaging for a cool, classy finish. It looks very elegant and is very easy to open.

Can this be the closure of the future? Time will tell. But I certainly see the Vino-Lok as the perfect closure: They are easily inserted and removed, they are reusable and recyclable, they have a consistent OTR, and are inert and therefore there is no risk of contamination. How perfect a closure is that?

∼

My friend exclaimed, "wine diamonds!" when he noticed tiny
crystals that looked like shards of glass as he poured the
white wine into my glass. They looked like anything
but diamonds. What were they?

WINE DIAMONDS ARE KNOWN by many different names including
tartrates, *tartrate crystals*, *cream of tartar* and *potassium bitartrate*.
Diamonds they are not, however—they sure will not make you rich,
though you can make a business out of them. In fact many have, as
these "diamonds" have been mined since the beginning of winemaking, though only isolated in 1769 by Swedish chemist Carl Wil-
helm Scheele (1742–1786), to make a wide array of products from
baking goods to medicines and industrial products, such as electro-
lytic tinning of iron and steel.

The crystals are a result of tartrate instability—that is, the result
of tartaric acid salification caused by the presence of potassium
mineral ions that triggers tartaric acid crystallization or simply tartrates. The heavy tartrates become insoluble in alcohol and at cold
temperatures, therefore, causing precipitation.

The most common form of tartrates is potassium bitartrate—
also known as *potassium acid tartrate* or *potassium hydrogen tartrate*,
the potassium acid salt of the dicarboxylic tartaric acid (dihydroxy-
succinic acid), due to the relativity higher concentration of potassium
in juice and wine though calcium tartrate can also happen. Potassium
bitartrate causes harmless clear crystals to form which can look
alarmingly similar to tiny shards of glass. If you have ever forgotten
a bottle of white wine at the back of the refrigerator and have dis-
covered crystals at the bottom then you have witnessed potassium
bitartrate crystallization.

The amount of tartrates that can form is greatest in wines with
high tartaric acid concentration, such as in a Riesling from a cool-
climate viticultural area, and depends on temperature, pH, and concentration of alcohol, potassium, calcium, and other compounds
such as phenols and proteins. Reds are less prone to tartrates because

of the lower tartaric acid and higher phenol concentrations. Phenols have an affinity for tartaric acid, therefore, partially inhibiting crystallization.

Although completely harmless, tartrates affect the appearance of wine because they form at the bottom of the bottle or on the face of the cork exposed to wine. In white wine, the crystals are colorless while in reds, the crystals absorb some red pigments from the wine and are therefore reddish in color. It is usually considered acceptable to find a small amount of tartrates in premium wines; however, the majority of wines are processed to safeguard against tartrates to alleviate any consumer concerns.

The process of protecting wine against tartrates is known as *cold stabilization* or *tartrate stabilization*, and involves chilling the wine at approximately or below (water) freezing for several days or more depending on the temperature. Larger wineries equipped with chilling units can cold stabilize wine in tanks right in the cellar. Tanks are equipped with an outer shell, known as a *cooling jacket*, filled with a running supply of refrigerated coolant, usually propylene glycol (food-grade antifreeze) to chill the wine. If you have ever noticed a thick layer of frost or ice around tanks when visiting wineries, you have witnessed cold stabilization.

It is a standard procedure though to first test cold stability before investing time, energy and money into chilling wine. This can be accomplished by either a conductivity test—quick but requires specialized equipment—or by placing a small wine sample in the refrigerator to establish if it throws crystals.

Where cold chilling is not possible, potassium bitartrate crystallization can be inhibited by adding metatartaric acid as is commonly done in home winemaking but not allowed in commercial wines in many winemaking regions of the world. Metatartaric acid is a dispersed polymer (hemipolyactide) of tartaric acid—meaning that it consists of many polymers with different molecular weights—obtained by heating tartaric acid above its melting point at 170°C

(338°F). Its drawback is that when added to wine, it hydrolyzes back to tartaric acid at a rate as a direct function of temperature and, therefore, loses effectiveness. Wines treated with metatartaric acid are meant to be drunk quickly particularly if they cannot be stored at cool temperatures.

Fascinating chemistry!

~

I have often heard red wine described as having a barnyard smell? Is that good or bad? And where does it come from?

WINES ARE OFTEN DESCRIBED as having a barnyard smell (or often a more vulgar word is used). Personal taste and preferences notwithstanding, if a barnyard aroma is subtle, it is considered acceptable and is often desired by many winemakers who assert that it adds complexity to certain styles of wines. But when the aromas are muted and overshadowed by a strong barnyard smell, then it is considered a fault. Such is the nature of the indigenous *Brettanomyces* yeast, more affectionately known as *Brett*; it can have both a positive influence on wine, for aficionados who are partial to it, or it can spoil wine outright. *Brettanomyces bruxellensis* yeast is the anamorph (non-sporulating form) of *Dekkera bruxellensis* yeast which causes like-it-or-not barnyard aromas, or medicinal, sweaty, "Band-Aid" and rancid odors that can be detected at very low concentrations in the hundreds of µg/L (parts per billion, or ppb) range. These are the results from three main compounds: 4-ethylphenol (4EP) and 4-ethylguaiacol (4EG), both usually referred to as *4EP/4EG*, and 3-methylbutyric acid, also known as *isovaleric acid.*

The challenge with *Brettanomyces* yeast is that it easily thrives throughout the winery and is difficult to eradicate, particularly that it seems to adapt to changing environments. It is an anaerobic microorganism, meaning that it thrives in the absence of oxygen. Specifically, it thrives in oak barrels feeding on cellulose or in wines with residual sugar, high pH or high polyphenol concentration. Red wines are inherently more susceptible to Brett owing to their higher pH and high polyphenol concentration. Residual sugar is usually not a problem in whites because they are well protected with sulfite when properly managed; in reds, however, where the style is meant to be a dry wine, residual sugar can be a source of food for Brett.

Eradicating *Brettanomyces* is nearly impossible except by stabilizing (membrane/sterile) filtration. But Brett is sensitive to free sulfur dioxide (from sulfite) and so it is easily preventable. The adage that "an ounce of prevention is worth a pound of cure" could not hold truer when it comes to Brett. So giddyap and hold that Brett lest you are partial to horses.

≈

What is the link between burnt rubber, cadavers, horse sweat and mice as it relates to winemaking?

"Um. It doesn't sound good *at all*." You are right.

These are all the result of spoilage from malolactic fermentation (MLF). The effects can be unsettling.

If MLF is not adequately controlled or is left to undesirable lactic acid bacteria, wine can acquire a wide range of off-flavors and odors ranging from burnt rubber to decayed meat. The list of culprit compounds—and particularly their common or chemical names—can be quite disconcerting to winemakers. Some compounds include putrescine, cadaverine, 4-ethylphenol (4EP), 4-ethylguaiacol (4EG), ethyl lactate, and ethyl tetrahydropyridine.

Putrescine and cadaverine are biogenic amines. Amines are organic compounds derived from the enzymatic decarboxylation of amino acids—that is, COO groups are removed from the COOH structures in the amino acids—and are the product of life processes and *biogenic* means that the compounds can induce physiological effects. Putrescine or butanediamine is derived from the decarboxylation of the amino acid arginine while cadaverine or penta-methylenediamine is derived from lysine. Both amines have a very strong, foul smell typical of decayed meat.

4-ethylphenol and 4-ethylguaiacol, commonly referred to as *4EP/4EG* as they usually co-exist, are phenolic compounds responsible for imparting horse-sweat and burnt rubber smells, respectively, and are the product of decarboxylation of hydroxycinnamic acids and their derivatives by *Brettanomyces bruxellensis* yeast. More specifically, 4EP and 4EG are the products of the decarboxylation of *p*-coumaric and ferulic acids and reduction of their intermediates.

And what is the major source of *p*-coumaric acid in Brett-affected wines? Toasted wood, and that is the reason why Brett occurs in wine aged in barrels, specifically, the root cause are lignin compounds in the oak wood which decompose when subjected to high toasting heat.

Ethyl lactate is the product of esterification—a reaction of a carbolic acid with an alcohol—of lactic acid, resulting from the malolactic conversion with ethyl alcohol, and imparts mild odors of butter and cream.

Ethyl tetrahydropyridine is an organic compound derived from piperidine which is a product of pyrine hydrogenation and which is responsible for imparting the smell of mouse nests or mouse urine and a mousey taste—none of which I have had the experience of smelling or tasting. (I am left to wonder who came up with those descriptors and the process but some things are best left unexplained.) The root cause in wine is not well understood but it is suspected to derive from bacterial spoilage including lactic acid bacteria.

Based on this evidence, you will clearly want to stay away from such spoilage-laced wines.

⟋⟍

Why can the use of sorbic acid be damaging to wines that have undergone malolactic fermentation?

WINES WITH RESIDUAL, FERMENTABLE sugars are prone to refermentation in the bottle if there are latent yeasts or bacteria that could spontaneously become active which should not be a concern in sterile-filtered wines.

Home winemakers safeguard against refermentation by adding sorbic acid in its salt form as potassium sorbate—a widely accepted food and beverage additive used to inhibit growth of yeast. Commercial wineries generally do not add potassium sorbate. Instead, they sterile filter wines to remove yeasts and bacteria.

Wine that has undergone malolactic fermentation will have a large population of lactic acid bacteria which will react with sorbic acid to produce hexadienol, otherwise known as *geraniol* which produces the strong and disagreeable odor of rotting geraniums—a highly undesirable outcome that cannot be reversed. It is simple to understand the result once we look at the chemical reaction. Sorbic acid is also known as *2,4-hexadienoic acid* and when it is decarboxylized—that is, a carbon atom is removed as a carbon dioxide molecule—the result is 3,7-dimethylocta-2,6-dien-1-ol, a monoterpenoid and an alcohol, better known as *hexadienol* or *geraniol*, a compound with a geranyl group (the geraniol functional group but lacking the hydroxyl group) that gives roses their beautiful scent and which is also found in geranium flowers. But in wine, the smell is repulsive and definitely a serious fault, one that points directly to a winemaking error.

~

My wine was crystal clear when I bottled it but then it suddenly turned cloudy. What happened?

PERFECTLY CRYSTAL-CLEAR WINES that have been properly fined and filtered can suddenly turn cloudy if not stabilized against proteins, especially when then subjected to warm temperatures.

Proteins are complex amino acid compounds essential to all living cells and are synthesized from raw materials, as in vines. Proteins are found in relatively high concentrations in grapes and remain soluble in white wine whereas tannins and color pigments in red wine will cause proteins to precipitate; protein concentration in white wine is therefore higher before stabilizing than in red wine.

Proteins are very sensitive to heat (think of egg white changing from colorless to white when heated) and in wine they can coagulate and cause a haze when temperature first rises high followed by a cool down. The extent of haze depends on temperature and protein concentration which can change throughout vinification due to changes in such physicochemical factors as alcohol concentration, temperature, and pH.

White wines, particularly varietals such as Sauvignon Blanc and Gewürztraminer that have a higher than normal concentration of proteins are at a higher risk and are much more susceptible to temperature variations, even in crystal-clear wine previously fined or filtered. Such wines are said to be protein or heat unstable and must be treated for protein stabilization. Wines with low phenolic concentration are also at risk, albeit much lower, whereas those aged in oak barrels have little risk.

Bentonite is the ideal fining agent to reduce protein concentration and achieve protein stability. Since it interacts with proteins, bentonite can be added to grape juice before fermentation, to an active fermentation or to wine at the end of fermentation. This process is known as *counterfining*.

Prevention is the best cure for protein haze as the condition is very difficult to reverse without affecting wine quality. The best advice then is to test must or wine for protein stability and counterfine accordingly or simply counterfine as a standard practice in whites or low phenolic reds.

Protein stability is determined using a heat stability test which should be performed at various stages of winemaking in high-risk wines, or at minimum, before bottling. A heat stability test consists of subjecting wine samples to a predetermined temperature for various durations. If a sample shows any sign of haze or precipitation, the juice or wine is not protein or heat stable and requires a bentonite treatment.

Once you have modified your winemaking to include protein stabilization, you may want to look at your wine storage environment and solve that source of heat. And if you decide to travel and drive across the Nevada desert with your newly acquired, prized bottles of premium Napa Valley wine, you may want to plan ahead and carry along a cooler.

~

Can I turn my spoiled wine into vinegar?

No, NOT UNLESS you like bad vinegar.

The idea of making vinegar—at least not the kind of good vinegar that would make mamma proud—from spoiled wine is a fallacy, although the word *vinegar* is derived from the Old French words *vin aigre* which means *sour wine*. To make good vinegar, you must start with good wine, not one tainted with volatile acidity (VA). And making good vinegar is not easy. Ask any vinegar maker.

The main component of vinegar is acetic acid, a weak acid belonging to the family of carboxylic acids. Therefore, because of its molecular structure, it is also known as *methanecarboxylic acid* and *ethanoic acid* which give us more clues as to how the acid is derived. The chemistry is actually quite simple if we were to look at the molecular structures of ethyl alcohol and acetic acid as well as the intermediate products.

If wine becomes overly exposed to air, aerobic acetic acid bacteria jump into action and start oxidizing ethanol which loses two hydrogen atoms to produce acetaldehyde—an aldehyde that imparts an off-putting smell. As acetaldehyde then oxidizes too, it gains an oxygen atom and the result is acetic acid which imparts the familiar vinegar smell in oxidized wine. The result is a vinegary wine—a blend of wine and some acetic acid—which is mediocre at best. Thinking that the subtle aromas and flavors are carried through unaffectedly from the wine to the vinegar is not correct.

Before acetic acid bacteria get to work, many other oxidizable compounds are altered and change the olfactory attributes and physicochemical nature of the wine; these are carried through to the vinegar. If the wine is in a very advanced state of oxidation, it will be laden with foul-smelling thiols and disulfides and who knows what other nasty compounds from other unknown yeasts or bacteria that may have taken residence in your "vinegar."

Vinegar, the good kind, is produced in a very controlled environment in a precise process of inoculating wine with acetic acid bacteria, which then ferments ethyl alcohol into acetic acid without any prior oxidation of other compounds.

So please! Make mamma proud and throw out that spoiled wine. If you want to make good vinegar for her, start with a good wine and do it the right way.

∿

I have taken all the necessary precautions in my winemaking but the wine is disappointingly exhibiting smells of rotten eggs and burnt rubber. What went wrong? How can I fix the problem?

HYDROGEN SULFIDE, often simply referred to as H_2S.

Hydrogen sulfide gas, a sulfide (meaning it has only one sulfur atom in its molecular structure), is colorless and toxic at high levels; it is actually added to natural gas (methane) to be able to detect leaks. Its main characteristic though is its strong and often repulsive odor found in, for example, sewers, bad breath, flatulence, and rotten eggs—not a healthy list of attributes. In wines, it is present in very small, non-toxic but easily detectable concentrations, in the 5 µg/L (ppb) range (in comparison, roughly two thousand times that amount is needed before eyes become irritated and other body functions are affected).

Hydrogen sulfide is a metabolic by-product of fermentation but usually rises to detectable levels in wine from fermentative yeasts that are overly stressed by such factors as excessive use of sulfur-based vineyard mildew and fungus inhibitors for crop-spraying (or if grapes are sprayed too close to harvest), excessive use of sulfites, nutrient deficiency during fermentation, reaction with sulfur deposits in oak barrels, and yeast strains (e.g., Montrachet) known to produce higher-than-normal levels of hydrogen sulfide.

In the presence of sulfur-containing amino acids, namely containing methionine and cysteine, sulfides can further give rise to thiols—a class of organic compounds similar to alcohols in molecular structure but have a sulfhydryl (sulfur–hydrogen) group instead of a hydroxyl (oxygen–hydrogen) group—and impart strong, often repulsive, odors akin to, for example, onions and garlic, burnt rubber, and rotten cabbage. When thiols oxidize the result is disulfides which, as the name implies, contain two sulfur atoms and are very difficult to deal with.

In winemaking, thiols are commonly referred to as *mercaptans*, though inappropriate as the later is derived from the Latin *mercurium captans* which translates to "mercury seizing."

Whatever the name though, eradicating sulfide smells can prove a challenge depending on concentrations; thiols cannot be eradicated without adversely affecting the chemistry and the quality of the wine.

If hydrogen sulfide is barely detectable, there is a good chance that it can be reduced and possibly eliminated by aerating the wine, such as by racking, given the low boiling point of pure hydrogen sulfide (−60.3°C or −76.5°F). This has the drawback of accelerating oxidation and has to be assessed against the severity of the problem. If hydrogen sulfide is very noticeable, the wine can be treated with a dilute one-percent copper sulfate solution. Copper sulfate reacts with hydrogen sulfide to form and precipitate copper sulfide which can be separated from the wine by racking or filtration.

Given the type of treatments required to attenuate the foul odors which may have limited success, clearly the best cure for sulfides is prevention.

~

My wine smells of sulfur. A winemaker told me to treat it with hydrogen peroxide—you know, the stuff to treat scratches and cuts. Is that safe?

THE SMELL IS ACTUALLY that of sulfur dioxide and when it is detectable in wine, it is considered a fault and points to overuse of sulfite in the winery. The culprit is free sulfur dioxide or free SO_2 which consists of molecular sulfur dioxide and sulfite and bisulfite ions. If the sulfur dioxide smell is minimal, one remedy is to aerate the wine by decanting if the smell is in the bottle. If the smell is in a large batch of wine, it can be racked into another container and where it can splash at the bottom. This will cause the free sulfur dioxide to combine with oxygen and become bound. But aerating bulk wine by splashing should be weighed against the potential negative impacts of other components of color, aromas, and flavors.

If there is no hurry in bottling the wine, it can be left to age in bulk. This will cause free sulfur dioxide to become bound and reduce the smell without adversely affecting quality.

If the wine needs to be bottled and the sulfur dioxide smell is quite pronounced, it can be safely removed using a three-percent hydrogen peroxide solution (the kind you can buy at the drug store), which reacts with the sulfite ions to produce sulfate ions.

But be careful! Hydrogen peroxide is a powerful oxidizer. If free sulfur dioxide has been totally consumed, adding hydrogen peroxide will cause oxidation of other wine components such as converting ethyl alcohol into acetaldehyde, a clear sign of wine oxidation recognizable as a nut-like smell akin to the smell of Sherry wine (where it is a virtue); and acetaldehyde also reduces the protective power of sulfur dioxide.

∾

Wines from the 2001 vintage in Ontario were known to smell uncharacteristically of asparagus and peanut. What caused this?

THE MULTICOLORED ASIAN LADY BEETLE (MALB).

MALB is a small, pesky beetle with the scientific name *Harmonia axyridis* but also known as *Japanese ladybug* and *Halloween lady beetle* (because they appear en masse in October). It is affectionately referred to as *ladybug* in Niagara's wine region where it caused some serious headaches in 2001. New York, Pennsylvania, Indiana and Minnesota, among other states were also affected.

MALBs are easily distinguished from other beetles of the same *Coccinellidae* family by their characteristic black, M-shaped marking on their pronotum—the dorsal plate of a beetle's prothorax which is located between the head and elytra (wing coverings on the main body).

H. axyridis is originally native to eastern Asia and has first been introduced into North America at the turn of the twentieth century with other kinds of beetles as predators to control crop-damaging insects. The beetles have proven very effective in controlling aphid populations and protecting crops in soybean fields. But in 2001 in the Niagara wine region, there was an alarmingly large population of ladybugs that, although great for soybean farmers, became the culprit of tainted, asparagus-smelling wine. And so it spawned much research and development in how to control MALB populations both in the vineyard and at the winery—yes, in wine.

In the vineyard, the little critters hid in grape clusters where they would go unnoticed if not controlled or treated with a recommended insecticide such as malathion or cypermethrin.

Malathion is a common organophosphate insecticide, chemically known as O,O-dimethyl phosphorothioate, which inhibits cholinesterase, an enzyme central to the proper functioning of the nervous system of insects (and humans too, although it is not considered toxic at the low doses used in fighting MALB or mosquitoes). Its drawback is that it is effective for approximately three days.

Cypermethrin is a pyrethroid insecticide—meaning that it belongs to a class of compounds synthesized from pyrethrum extract obtained from chrysanthemum plants —with a faster-acting neurotoxin that is effective for seven days or more. Cypermethrin is commonly found in household insecticides such as Raid®.

Would you like to know the IUPAC chemical name for cypermethrin?

(R,S)-alpha-cyano-3-phenoxybenzyl(1RS)-cis,trans-3-(2,2-dichlorovinyl)-2,2-dimethylcyclopropane-carboxylate. If you really feel challenged, try drawing its molecular structure.

At harvest at the winery's grape-receiving area, ladybugs get crushed and pressed into the juice—yucky! Winemakers who knew about the problem tried various solutions to eradicate the ladybugs from their crop. There were those who hired extra help to sort grapes on a conveyor-operated sorting table and weed out the pesky critters, but that was a lot of work and not efficient. Today, there are shaker tables to make this effective. Then there was the winemaker who dumped the uncrushed grapes into a bin, which he then filled with water. Genial idea at first as the critters floated to the surface and could easily be sieved out. The problem was that the grapes retained substantial water at the crusher, which diluted the wine.

Let's look at the creepy but fascinating chemistry of beetles.

MALBs, as with many coccinellids, possess a defense mechanism—as in when they are agitated or crushed—known as *reflex bleeding* whereby they secrete methoxypyrazine chemicals, chief among these is 2-isopropyl–3-methoxypyrazine (IPMP), a foul-smelling, yellow-orange fluid which is also found in and released from the "blood" of the beetles. Methoxypyrazines are compounds part of a group of pyrazine chemicals responsible for imparting, for example, a vegetative, herbaceous aroma in Sauvignon Blanc and Cabernet Sauvignon where it is often described as a bell-pepper aroma. The specific chemical compound here is 3-isobutyl–2-methoxypyrazine (IBMP) which is also prominent in wines made from unripe grapes. Although there are no health concerns, MALB-secreted IPMP imparts objectionable peanut and asparagus aromas, detectable in the low ng/L (ppt) range—the equivalent of a drop in an Olympic-sized swimming pool.

Research published in 2004 and led by Dr. Gary Pickering at the Cool Climate Oenology and Viticulture Institute (CCOVI) at Brock University in St. Catharines, Ontario demonstrated that a single beetle in one liter (approximately a quarter of a gallon) of wine had a small but detectable negative impact on aromas. Although the wine exhibited aromas of asparagus, bell pepper, and peanut, there was minimal impact on flavors. However, at ten beetles per liter, desirable aromas were severely muted by high asparagus, bell pepper, and peanut aromas *and* flavors. Interesting research.

For now, there is no known effective cure to eliminate methoxy-pyrazines from wines but the smell can be masked to some extent depending on concentration by using an oak treatment, for example, by macerating oak chips or cubes in the affected wine. In the vineyard, insecticides such as cypermethrin and malathion have been proposed but have a limited effectiveness period before beetles reinfest a vineyard considering that current research demonstrates that even dead beetles can taint wine—up to six days post-mortem.

And so in the meantime, I guess we will need Dr. Pickering to continue his research.

The Multicolored Asian Lady Bug, or MALB (*top*); MALBs in a grape cluster (*bottom*). *Photos courtesy of Prof. Gary Pickering, Brock University. Top photograph by T. Tolasch.*

Wine Service

~

Wine appreciation is often described as snobbish. Who can blame the critics? After all, serious aficionados can spend considerable time swirling that lusciously *über*wine in their mouths before they swallow and then describing it with endless poetic prose, speaking of the wine as being fruit-forward and stylish with intertwined layers of sweet exotic fruit, a soupçon of black currant and oodles of *frutta di bosco* aromas framed by subtle earthy flavors, buttressed with firm though well-integrated tannins and a lingering finish. Then there is that whole bottle uncorking, decanting, and serving ritual that one must consider.

In this section, we will examine some topics of practical importance on the science of wine service and appreciation and demystify certain rituals.

Do Riedel glasses really make a difference in the taste of wine? Should wine be decanted? And what is all the fuss about choosing the "right" wine for specific foods?

Read on.

What is the difference between bitterness and astringency?

BITTERNESS IS A TASTE and astringency is a sensation.

Our tongue consists of many types of taste buds, each sensing or perceiving different flavors. They can discern four primary tastes or flavors: sweetness, saltiness, acidity, and bitterness. It has always been maintained that these flavors were detected on specific areas of the tongue: sweetness is detected at the tip, saltiness on the sides towards the front, acidity on the sides towards the back, and bitterness at the back of the tongue. The science of taste now defines a fifth taste, *umami*, a Japanese word meaning "savory" which can be found in high-protein content foods or those containing glutamates (glutamic acid) such as food treated with monosodium glutamate (MSG). Recent research now postulates that these five primary flavors can be detected all over the tongue.

In wine, bitterness and astringency are due to tannin, a phenolic compound found in the skin, stems and seeds of grapes or which can also be imparted through the use of oak barrels during the maturation process or through the addition of tannin derivative products. Tannin is what determines body in wine and an important element in the overall structure and flavor profile. High tannin concentration can make a wine overly bitter, even astringent, giving a puckery, dry sensation in the mouth akin to drinking strong, unsweetened tea.

∾

What is the scientific basis for recommending red wine with red meat and white with fish? Can you recommend how best to pair food and wine?

PAIRING RED WINE WITH RED MEAT and white with fish have been the accepted, long-standing traditions based on two classical, simple food and wine pairing principles. First, red wines had been traditionally quite tannic which as we have seen, can be made to feel softer on the palate by pairing with protein-based food such a red meat. Then, fish is best paired with whites because of the higher acidity that tends to attenuate those peculiar fish smells and flavors; tannins in red would simply make fish taste "metallic."

But those principles were "instituted" long ago. With the plethora of wine styles, varietals and blends from all over the world, and with the ever-evolving fusion of cuisines, those principles are now only general guidelines. To match wine to food, you really need to consider the type of food, the way it is prepared, and the kind of sauce or seasoning used. And if you want to match wine to food, then you need to know something about the wine.

What varietal or blend is it? Was it aged in oak barrels? Is it tannic? What about acidity and alcohol?

The basic guiding principle here is to pair food and wine to complement each other. In other words, they should not clash and with no one food or wine component dominating. By complementing each other, we mean that flavors can enhance one another or can create a contrast.

What is important here is that food and beverages should not disrupt the delicate balance of the five tastes we detect on our tongue which would otherwise make those unappealing. That is because the five tastes counteract each other. For example, acidity reduces the perception of sweetness but reinforces bitterness. Flavors must exist in harmony to deliver great taste for an enjoyable experience. If any element is not in balance, our senses quickly detect the imbalance and our experience diminishes. We salt food, add tangy sauces, sugar and other flavor enhancers to achieve balance and enjoy the taste. We add sugar or milk or both to coffee to reduce bitterness which is also why it is usually served with dessert.

Now then, when we say that food and wine should complement each other and should not clash, this really means that these should not disrupt that balance and that they should appeal to our likes stored in our brains.

Let's look at some specific examples—some classical, some modern—of good food and wine pairings and examples of poor or disagreeable pairings.

Champagne or any other brut (dry) sparkling wine pairs well with shellfish or caviar, but not bitter chocolate. The high acidity (and imperceptible sweetness) in these bubblies is a delectable contrast to the saltiness of the food. However, acidity reinforces bitterness making such wines a disagreeable pairing with bitter chocolate. Sweet chocolate would make a better pairing as acidity and sweetness now create a palatable contrast. In fact, this is why lightly sweet Riesling, Gewürztraminer or even a rosé pair well with Asian food and why Stilton cheese is paired with Port wine or Roquefort with Sauternes. Keep in mind that spicy foods augment the hot sensation of alcohol so choose a low-alcohol wine for those.

Try a full-bodied Chardonnay with lobster or pasta with a cream sauce. The richness of Chardonnay and cream sauce enhance one another.

A red Burgundy or other Pinot Noir would be an excellent match with salmon steak in a mushroom sauce. The earthiness of the sauce and delicate taste of salmon complement equally delicate Pinot Noirs.

Choose a bold, rich, full-bodied Cabernet Sauvignon or Bordeaux-style red with rich, high-fat or high-protein food such as that hearty, Angus beef steak. Here you need those tannins to cut through the fat and those powerful aromas and flavors that can stand up to the rich flavors of such food. Speaking of fat, this explains the traditional pairing of foie gras (seared, pâté, or *au torchon*, i.e., prepared and wrapped in a tight bundle in a cheesecloth or linen dishtowel) with Sauternes. And for something new, try foie gras with an Ontario Icewine.

Then there are some foods or ingredients that simply make wine pairing difficult or outright impossible. Onions, garlic, spicy ingredients and vinegar-based dressings are very difficult to pair because they can easily overpower wine so always go easy on these ingredients.

But asparagus and brussels sprouts are sworn enemies of wine. Why? Chemistry provides the answers. Asparagus contains methionine, a sulfur-containing amino acid that, when it degrades, such as by cooking, produces methanethiol, or methyl mercaptan— a thiol compound that smells of rotten cabbage. The green, vegetal smell of asparagus will make wine taste metallic and green. Oaked Chardonnay and tannic wines are known to be no match for asparagus. However, Sauvignon Blanc and Pinot Grigio are two white varietals known to be able to stand up to the vegetable. The off-putting smell can also be attenuated by using a sauce, such as Hollandaise. Brussels sprouts too are a problem. They contain phenyl-thiocarbamide, a bitter-tasting substance that makes wine pairing an impossible challenge and also contain precursor compounds that give rise to foul-smelling sulfides and disulfides.

Now, I never had wine with eggs—my intake of eggs is limited to breakfast—but my curiosity was piqued when I read that along with asparagus and brussels sprouts, eggs too are considered an enemy of wine. Interesting because egg whites are loaded with proteins—which would go well with tannic red wines if you are into raw egg whites—but the proteins are broken down once heated, and therefore become fairly neutral when paired with wine. The problem lies in the yolk; it is rich in fats and oils which will create a coating in the mouth and essentially act as a barrier to flavors.

Then there is the case of artichokes. There, the culprit compound is cynarin, a very complex acid that imparts a sweet taste—without the sugar—and which is more soluble in alcohol; the net effect is that wine will seem somewhat flabby due to the perceived lower acidity.

Now, all this talk about wine and food has made me hungry. I will go and have a sandwich and explore the pairing opportunities between prosciutto and Italian wines.

~

Why are some wines stored in clear-glass bottles while others are in brown- or green-colored glass?

WINE IS SENSITIVE TO THE DAMAGING rays of light, particularly ultraviolet (UV) rays from sunlight and fluorescent lighting. That is why wine (and beer which is in fact a lot more sensitive because of the isohumulones found in the hops) is packaged in dark bottles—the best example is Port in those familiar, dark, opaque bottles. Wines packaged in clear-glass bottles are meant for quick consumption and should be stored in carton boxes until you are ready to drink them.

Again, there is some interesting physics and chemistry at play here in what is known as *light-strike reactions* which can impart corn chip or asparagus off-odors to wine, what the French call *goût de lumière*—literally "taste of light."

All forms of radiation, including visible light, UV and X rays, have energy that is directly proportional to their frequencies or inversely proportional to their wavelengths—that is, high-frequency waves have short wavelengths and vice versa. And the greater the energy, the greater the catalytic effect of chemical reactions in wine.

Of concern in wine is visible light and the sun's UVA rays—yes, UVA rays because research has proven that even a short exposure of wine to sun (UVB and UVC are absorbed by the atmosphere) in the order of hours can have detrimental effects. That is because UVA rays lie in the 315–400 nanometer (nm) range of the electromagnetic spectrum and, therefore, has more energy than visible light which lies in the 400–700 nm range.

Glass acts as a filter but clear glass offers no protection against UVA and visible light. Green glass offers some protection but only half as well as amber. Dark-amber glass offers almost complete protection.

So why is so much wine, particularly many of the ultra-premium wines of the world, packaged in green glass? This is likely for historical reasons when making green-colored glass was easiest and the effect of radiation on wine was unknown.

But glass is only half the story. We must now consider the optical properties of wine to then determine how radiation effects any chemical reaction.

Research has shown that wavelengths in the 375–440 nm range, i.e., the high end of the UVA range and the blue (low) end of the visible light range, are most damaging to wine. The amount of radiation absorbed by wine in this range is directly proportional to opacity, therefore, red wine absorbs the most and is most affected while white wine absorbs the least—rosé wine is in the middle. As such, for marketing purposes where displaying color is important, white wine can be stored in clear glass, although not for extended periods of time. That is why premium whites such as age-worthy Chablis wines come in dead-leaf-colored glass, a golden-yellow color that provides better protection than green.

Opaque, deeply colored, rich reds absorb almost all radiation, however, these have the highest concentration of effect-inhibiting tannins which provide protection. But if the concentration is low or the extent of exposure is long, unpleasant and off-putting aromas and flavors can develop. Specifically, red wine has sulfur-containing amino acids, namely, methionine and cysteine which have a thiol (sulfur–hydrogen) side chain in their structures. These then react with naturally occurring vitamins, such as riboflavin (vitamin B_2) and pantothenic acid (vitamin B_5)—water-soluble vitamins that are easily destroyed by heat, oxygen and, that is right, UV light. The products of this reaction are sulfur compounds such as hydrogen sulfide, dimethyl sulfide (DMS), and dimethyl disulfide (DMDS)—all responsible for imparting a range of foul smells from rotten eggs to cabbage and wet dog.

Now I am left to wonder if my magnum (1.5-liter bottle) of 1991 Château d'Yquem, in a clear-glass bottle that I bought for my son born that same year was affected by X rays on its travel from the U.S. It was pre-9/11, however, the unyielding airport security guard simply could not be convinced not to X-ray my precious bottle. I had plans for foie gras with the Yquem but I am afraid that corn chips will be a better pairing now.

~

I must often store a bottle of unfinished wine. What is the best way to do that?

IF YOU ARE LOOKING FOR a repeat performance from that wonderful bottle you had with last evening's dinner, there are several ways to store the unfinished wine though the wine will most likely be different from the first few sips you imbibed.

As soon as a bottle is opened, the wine becomes exposed to air and oxygen starts acting on it very slowly. Depending on the type of wine and its age, the wine can actually smell and taste differently even after say fifteen minutes in the glass. The transformation is usually a beneficial one, however, leave the wine in a partially filled bottle and it can start taking on a different color or different aromas and so this is never recommended.

There are several ways and gadgets to store wine—some work better than others.

In my experience, using a canister of nitrogen gas with a special bottle attachment to dispense wine works best as any leftover wine is protected with the gas. The bottle can be stored separately in the refrigerator without the tank. The drawback is that it is somewhat bulky at the dinner table and certainly does not look elegant.

Probably the most effective way to store an unfinished bottle is using a blend of inert gas dispensed from a can such as Private Reserve™. This is similar to the procedure in wineries where partially filled tanks are purged with argon, nitrogen or carbon dioxide gas or a blend such as beer gas (a blend of carbon dioxide and nitrogen). The process is simple. Attach the supplied spray tube to the can nozzle, insert the tube in the bottle and just above the wine surface, and spray for a few seconds while holding the cork in position ready to insert it as you remove the tube. You can keep the wine for several days.

Another trick is to pour leftover wine into a smaller bottle, ideally first sparged with inert gas and then recork; the idea is to reduce the amount of air that is allowed to interact with the wine.

Placing an unfinished bottle in a refrigerator does *not* help, in fact, wine takes up more oxygen at colder temperatures. To keep that unfinished bottle of white chilled for the next day, it is best to sparge it with inert gas, recork it and then place it in the refrigerator.

One last gadget that seems popular, albeit controversial in its effectiveness is the vacuum pump. By placing a special rubber closure with a one-way valve on the bottle, air can be drawn out with the special pump and protect wine under a vacuum.

Does it *really* work? In my experience, again, I have found this device to work relatively well. It can preserve wine for a couple of days. My only problem is that the vacuuming action draws out some of the volatile aromas and so the wine cannot possibly smell the same even the next day. Give it a test try—stick your nose close to the pump as you are pumping air out; you will smell aromas which means that they are, in fact, getting out.

And what about preserving those precious bubbles in an unfinished bottle of bubbly?

No, the old trick of placing the handle of a teaspoon—some say a silver teaspoon—in the neck of a bottle does *not* work. There is no scientific explanation to support the claim that the teaspoon prevents loss of gas and it has been experimentally disproved. The best way to preserve bubbles though there is always some loss is to use a closure specially designed for carbonated-drink bottles. The closure fits over the neck of the bottle and two "arms" are swiveled under the collar to keep the closure in place. Never place a cork or other unsecured closure in the neck; it will eventually fly off under the gas pressure.

Undoubtedly, the best solution is to share and finish the bottle with your partner or a friend over a nice meal.

Why worry about preserving wine?

What temperature should I be serving wine?

I MUST ADMIT I CRINGED the time when a party host tossed my bottle of full-bodied Maleta Winery Gamay Noir in the fridge. But that little faux pas pales in comparison to the time a restaurant server decided to cool down my glass of tepid rosé with a scoopful of ice.

Wine served at the "wrong" temperature is not a matter of etiquette; it makes wine downright unpleasurable and perhaps even undrinkable. Heed those recommendations calling for a wine to be served *chilled, well chilled,* or at *room temperature.* The temperature in a refrigerator can vary between 0° and 8°C (32° and 46°F); and "room temperature" is a carry-over from the old days when room temperature was closer to 18°C (64°F) then it is to today's where it can range between 20° and 24°C (68° and 75°F). A simple range for all wines is not really helpful and can make you miss out on wine pleasure. There is no single fit-all rule on wine service temperature. Every type and style of wine should be served at the "right" temperature for full enjoyment and appreciation. This is not snobbery and the science of smell and taste can help us better appreciate the need to serve wine at the right temperature.

Cold temperatures tend to mute delicate aromas and flavors and enhance the perception of acidity—the greater the perception of acidity, the lower the perception of sweetness. But acidity also reinforces bitterness and astringency and so by commutation the colder the temperature, the stronger the effects of bitterness and astringency.

Let's look at specific styles and recommended serving temperatures knowing that, in general, whites have relatively higher acidity than reds but almost no tannins. These recommendations are from Master of Wine (MW) Jancis Robinson's *Wine Course.* (MWs are internationally recognized individuals who have undergone rigorous training and examination. There are currently 277 worldwide.)

Light, dry aromatic whites, such as Sauvignon Blanc, Muscat, Riesling, and Gewürztraminer are best enjoyed when served at 8°–

12°C (46°–54°F) for the acidity to be refreshing but not so cold as to mute those aromas. If the same whites are made in a sweeter style, chill them several degrees downward to 5°–10°C (41°–50°F) to enhance the acidity and better balance the sweetness. At the opposite end of the white wine service spectrum, full-bodied dry whites such as oak-aged Chardonnay which have lower acidity and some tannin should be served at 12°–16°C (54°–61°F). Any style in between including rosés should be served at 10°–12°C (50°–54°F); chill a little more if it is a sweeter-style wine.

Sparkling wines also have high acidity and delicate aromas and flavors; a colder temperature in the range 6°–10°C (43°–50°F) will show the bubbles best—the very fine bubbles will favorably slowly release the aromas.

Light, fruity, dry reds such as a Beaujolais-style Gamay should be served at 10°–12°C (50°–54°F) since these have very little tannin content and would want the acidity and fruit to shine through. Many will recommend serving these wines, particularly Beaujolais Nouveau, from an ice bucket. As tannin content increases, medium-bodied reds are best enjoyed at 14°–17°C (57°–63°F) while full-bodied reds such as a complex Pinot Noir or a richly concentrated Cabernet should be served at 15°–18°C (59°–64°F).

To achieve these temperatures, first become acquainted with your refrigerator's temperature profile.

What temperature is it at, and how different is it in various areas, i.e., top shelf vs. back of the shelf, door shelf, etc.? Then determine how long it takes to chill a bottle to the desired temperature. Repeat the same procedure with a bucket of ice for those occasions when you will need to chill a bottle quickly when guests show up unexpectedly. But, please! Never toss ice into wine.

Should I decant wine before serving?

IF YOU WANT TO STIR UP some controversy, ask the question at your next wine tasting event.

Decanting involves transferring wine from a bottle to a glass decanter to either let the wine "breathe" before serving or to separate the wine from sediments. (Wines other than reds and Port are not expected to throw a deposit.) There is now a plethora of aerating or "breathing" gadgets for sale that emulate decanting without the need for a decanter.

Reds and particularly old or premium wines and Port wines will throw a light or heavy deposit, a natural and normal (expected) phenomenon and the result of wine aging. While pouring, the sediment would most likely be shaken back into suspension, making the wine cloudy and taste quite bitter with an overwhelming puckery feeling in the mouth. To avoid such problems the wine should be decanted, preferably through a decanting sieve. This practice is straightforward and non-controversial but the same cannot be said of "letting the wine breathe." Some believe that the wine should be allowed to "breathe," which really means that it needs to oxygenate to demonstrate its full potential and array of complex aromas and flavors but others claim that it does nothing or that the wine is sufficiently oxygenated while being poured into a glass.

Not being one to pass up on an opportunity to contribute to the science of wine and wine tasting, I undertook a very simple experiment to validate the chemistry of oxidation–reduction reactions and demonstrate if decanting has any effect on wine aromas and flavors. I took three identical bottles of eight-year-old homemade Cabernet Sauvignon—the finest in my cellar. One bottle was decanted four hours before the scheduled taste test; a second bottle was opened and some wine poured into a glass half an hour before the tasting. At tasting time, wine from the decanter was poured into a glass; the third bottle was uncorked and wine poured into a glass. The three wines were then compared for aromas and flavors. The wines were as can be expected not dramatically different, however, there were some notable differences. The wines showed a touch more complexities with longer exposure to air—that is to say, the wine in the decanter showed best. The extent of differences is obviously a function of the type and age of wine but there are differences nonetheless. (See page 152 for another experiment on decanting that demonstrates different results.)

Are the subtleties worth all the decanting fuss? Well, that is really all in the opinion of the "glassholder." But at your next dinner party, taste wine and let it sit in the glass for even ten minutes before your next sip and see if you can detect any change and if you want to stir controversy, ask everyone to do the same.

And what about those aerating gizmos? I could not detect a difference and, in any case, the action of pouring wine into a glass would provide as much aeration as the gizmo.

You be the judge.

∽

A glass for Bordeaux, one for Montrachets, one for Burgundies, and on and on. Why so many different styles of stemware? Do they make any difference?

ABSOLUTELY, BUT—there has to be a *but*—is there really a difference between two similarly shaped glasses, for example, one for Bordeaux reds and one for Syrahs?

Our noses and palates all have different thresholds for detecting aromas and flavors. Those that have acute sensorial abilities claim to be able to tell the difference between two similarly shaped glasses. After all, it is believed that humans can sense thousands of different smells (compared to only five tastes). Differently shaped glasses, though, definitely express wine differently.

Several years ago I had the opportunity to participate in a enlightening wine tasting event hosted by Georg Riedel, the tenth-generation glass-maker from the family that revolutionized wine tasting technology, along with Michael Mondavi, then CEO of the Robert Mondavi Corp., and Donald Ziraldo, co-founder of Inniskillin Wines Inc. Surely this was an opportunistic marketing event, however, the objective was to demonstrate the effects of glass shape on wine tasting and what better way to do it than sipping Robert Mondavi wines and Inniskillin Icewines in Riedel glasses.

The demonstration involved tasting a wine in a *joker* glass— your standard cylindrical goblet on a stem—and then in two Riedel glasses, one designed specifically for the type of wine being tasted and another one for some other type of wine. The differences were unbelievable; even my highly skeptical friends could not believe it. Yes, the Cabernet Sauvignon showed best in the Bordeaux glass, the Pinot Noir in the Burgundy glass, the Chardonnay in the Montrachet glass, and the Cabernet Franc Icewine was simply awesome in the specially designed Riedel Inniskillin Icewine glass.

How would one explain what is happening?

Wine contains hundreds of volatile aromatic compounds in different concentrations which we can detect with and without swirling the glass. The shape and size of the stemware affect how the aromas are concentrated and blended when we smell the wine as well as how and where the flavors are delivered to the palate when tasting. The purpose of swirling our wine glass is to volatize those aromas and flavors so that our senses can detect them.

An important note about bubbly: sparkling wine should be served in tall flutes—not those old Champagne *coupes* purportedly modeled after the breasts of Madame de Pompadour, the (in)famous mistress of King Louis XV of France or of Queen of France Marie Antoinette, though neither is probably true. Ensure that the flutes are properly dried with a cloth—never pour sparkling wine into a glass rinsed with water; water droplets will dramatically inhibit bubbles. Also, never swirl sparkling wine in the flute; winemakers worked long and hard to get all those bubbles into the wine. Swirling the glass would cause the bubbles to dissipate prematurely and therefore reducing the experience of the wine. There is no need to swirl the glass to smell the aromas; the bubbles do all the work—as they rise up through the wine they "carry" aromas to our nose or as researchers Liger-Belair et al. described, "... the rising and collapsing bubbles act as a continuous paternoster lift for aromas ..." by bursting into "hundreds of tiny liquid jets every second, which quickly break up into a multitude of tiny droplets." These researchers and scientists at the Université de Reims Champagne-Ardenne, Université de Bourgogne, and the German Research Center for Environmental Health were tasked in proving scientifically that the tiny droplets did in fact bear all those wonderful aromas—or what they call *aerosols*—as the bubbles rise to the surface and burst. According to their findings published in the *Proceedings of the National Academy of Sciences*, they used an advanced ultrahigh-resolution mass spectrometry technique known as *FT-ICR-MS (Fourier Transform Ion Cyclotron Resonance Mass Spectrometer)* to discriminate a multitude of compounds released as bubbles burst and which possessed organoleptic properties.

Interesting research. Snobbery? I think not. Give it a try—but please do not swirl the glass.

~

What is the best way for removing red wine stains from a tablecloth or a carpet?

OH! THOSE PESKY RED WINE stains on white tablecloths or a Persian carpet can send a dinner party into a frenzied debate over the best way to remove a stain, ranging from pouring salt—some will even argue that Kosher salt works best—over the stain, to pouring white wine, to using specially-formulated products. There are entire websites dedicated to solving this problem, again with a most unusual and varied array of products and techniques, from the simple to the elaborate. A little chemistry knowledge of red wine and material properties should help us figure this one out. But as we can expect, every material will probably require a different treatment.

Red stains are caused by anthocyanins, the red pigment compounds present in red wine only. The ability to remove the stain then relies on the ability to lift or dissolve the anthocyanins from the material. But we know that anthocyanins dissolve better in water than in alcohol. To lift the stain then requires a solvent with molecules capable of bonding with the anthocyanin molecules, and that bond needs to be stronger than the bond between the anthocyanins and the compounds in the stained material. Here are some solvents and techniques that should do the trick and which are recommended on websites.

On a cotton or polyester tablecloth or on carpets, first blot—not scrub—the stain with an absorbent *white* cloth or paper towel. Avoid colored cloths that might otherwise transfer color to the tablecloth or carpet. Pour water over the stain and blot again, and repeat until the stain disappears as much as possible. At this point, you can toss the tablecloth into the wash; what is important is to not allow the stain to dry. Alternatively, you can sprinkle some salt over the stain, allow the salt to absorb the water and stain, and then follow the same procedure as above. Salt attracts water in wine by osmosis and thus pulls away the water-soluble anthocyanins.

Alternatively, you can use a strong oxidizing agent such as hydrogen peroxide—the kind you store in your pharmacy—or better still, sodium percarbonate. Sodium percarbonate or sodium carbonate peroxide, both synonyms for sodium carbonate peroxyhydrate and commonly referred to as *percarbonate*, is a granular-form caustic cleaning agent produced from sodium carbonate through chemical bonding with hydrogen peroxide. It is the active ingredient in many laundry cleaning products. Oxidizing agents work by chemically reacting with the stain to change its color, which can then be washed with water. Use a dilute solution of hydrogen peroxide on carpets weaved from natural fibers and use a dilute solution of sodium percarbonate on carpets weaved from synthetic fibers. Be sure to test on a small inconspicuous area before treating stains to ensure that the treatment does not adversely affect the fibers or colors of the carpet. Following the treatment, wet the stain with water and blot with a white cloth and let dry or in the case of a tablecloth, toss into the washing machine.

How well do these solvents and techniques work? I have put the techniques and one commercial product to test to determine how well these would perform. I spotted a cotton tablecloth with red wine. I treated one spot with water, a second with salt followed by water, a third spot with pharmacy-grade hydrogen peroxide, another with a commercial solution (whose chemical ingredients were not listed), and the last spot with a concentrated sodium percarbonate solution. The latter performed best by a mile. The concentrated solution of sodium percarbonate effectively removed the stain upon application whereas all other required a machine wash to remove.

So, unless you want to have to remove everything from the tablecloth to toss it into the washing machine, you may want to simply stock up on a little sodium percarbonate. You will be able to treat the stain quickly and efficiently without having to disrupt the whole dinner party and you will silence your audience with your astute stain-removing skills.

～

How do I saber a bottle of Champagne?

WE ARE NOT SUGGESTING or recommending that you try this at home—this is actually very dangerous, especially if you are not familiar with sparkling wine chemistry and bottle physics. Many how-to videos have surfaced on *YouTube*, some providing a demonstration without explaining the proper technique.

Consider the case of American gold-medal skier Lindsey Vonn

who wanted to spray the crowd with a bottle of Champagne to celebrate her event victory in Val d'Isère, France in February 2009. She ended up requiring surgery on her right thumb after she slashed a tendon from the sharp glass—this after someone decided to "saber" the bottle with the sharp edge of a ski.

The technique of "uncorking" a bottle of Champagne with a saber is known as *sabrage*, and according to one legend, the practice is believed to have originated with Napoleon (Bonaparte) and his army to celebrate military victories in post-French Revolution France and that is when he declared that "Champagne! In victory one deserves it; in defeat one needs it." But according to a local and completely opposite legend, after Napoleon was defeated the Champagne region was occupied by Russian troops and the officers faced with caves full of bottles could not be bothered to open them by hand and used their saber instead.

Whatever the legend, a master champenois "saberer" will make the art of sabrage look deceivingly simple as if slicing effortless through thin air. The glass is not sliced. Instead, the saber is used to knock off the collar—the top portion of the glass, just under the lip where the wire cage or muselet rests. This technique is very dangerous in the hands of amateurs. It requires know-how, skill and deft abilities.

To saber a bottle of bubbly, it must first be well chilled. This serves two purposes. It minimizes foaming and loss of precious wine (you will recall that the pressure of a gas decreases with decreasing temperature) and, more importantly, it ensures a clean cut—a warm bottle could cause the glass to shatter in your hand.

Before sabering, remove the foil or capsule as well as the neck label if any which holds the bottom of the foil onto the glass. If you are experienced in sabering bottles of bubbly and work quickly, you can simply remove the wire cage and proceed with sabering. Alternatively, you can untwist the wire cage and move it up and twist it again into position just above the bottom lip of the bottle;

this will avoid injuring your spectators if the cork ejects prematurely.

Now, the more important and trickier steps of sabrage—locate the seam on either side of the bottle; it runs the length of the bottle. Using a saber or some other sharp object such as a heavy-duty kitchen knife, you will need to knock off the top portion of the bottle where the seam and top portion connect.

To saber, hold the bottle in the left hand at a forty-five-degree angle with the cork pointing up and away from people. From approximately halfway on the bottle using a smooth upward motion run the saber *along the seam* to the top portion. The cork and collar will fly off with a little foaming and absolutely no glass falls into the bottle.

Pour the wine into Champagne flutes—do not be tempted to drink straight out of the bottle. If you ever plan to attend a frat party, leave the bubbly and saber at home. Please! You may instead want to try and quiz your frat buddies on the names of the various sizes of Champagne bottles if you need some safe and cheap entertainment. Try it yourself—answers are at the end of this Q&A.

If sabering is not for you and you prefer to uncork a bottle of bubbly the traditional way, you might be interested to know that there is a little bit of science involved here too, specifically, physics. After removing the capsule and wire cage, place the bottom of the bottle in your right hand and hold the cork tightly with the left fingers. While holding the bottle at a forty-five-degree angle and pointing away from people, twist the bottle with the *right* hand— not the left hand—while applying pressure with both hands towards each other to prevent the cork from popping too quickly. Pulling a cork out too quickly can result in gushing, loss of precious bubbles, and wine all over the floor (keep your pets away too). Keep the left hand steady and tight and continue to twist with the right hand until the cork comes free. Continue holding the bottle at an angle; this minimizes foaming and gushing. Then slowly start pouring into glasses or set the bottle gently on the table. When done properly there should be a very faint, barely audible swish and not a pop.

So what is different from untwisting the cork with the left hand? The diameter of the cork is much smaller than that of the bottom of the bottle and, therefore, twisting the bottom increases torque which makes uncorking that much easier.

And remember—always point a sparkling wine bottle away from people while uncorking or sabering. The cork can fly at bubbly speeds in excess of 50 km/h (30 mph).

So were you able to list the names of the various sizes of Champagne bottles? Here they are: a *quarter bottle* contains 187 mL, a *half bottle* is 375 mL, the standard *bottle* is 750 mL or approximately 25 fl oz, a *magnum* is 1.5 liters or the equivalent of two standard bottles, a *jeroboam* is 3 liters or the equivalent of four bottles, a *rehoboam* is 4.5 liters or the equivalent of six bottles, a *methuselah* is 6 liters or the equivalent of eight bottles, a *salmanazar* is 9 liters or the equivalent of twelve bottles, a *balthazar* is 12 liters or the equivalent of sixteen bottles, and a *nebuchadnezzar* is 15 liters or the equivalent of twenty bottles—now that is one serious, giant bottle and way too unwieldy to even consider sabering.

∾

Winecraft or Witchcraft?

~

IT IS OFTEN SAID THAT WINEMAKING is part art and part science. Surely any craft as old and as intriguing as winemaking holds an element of artistry but when the expression of personal convictions and scientifically unsubstantiated claims blur the line between art and science, the art can sometimes border on the paranormal and the science on witchcraft. The huge disparities in beliefs and winemaking methods, now coupled with the green movement and sustainable agricultural practices, have created diametrically opposed camps in winemaking philosophy.

This extends to wine appreciation too. Gizmos and gadgets flooding the market and which promise to enhance the wine tasting experience seem to be taking a life of their own.

So how serious is biodynamic farming and winemaking?

Does the cycle of the moon affect winemaking?

Do "wine enhancers" or wine magnets alter or improve wine?

These are a few of the topics discussed in this section.

What is the difference between organic and biodynamic wines? How are these different from those produced from sustainable winemaking?

ORGANIC AND BIODYNAMIC WINES are nothing new; it can be argued that the concepts are as ancient as winemaking at a time when there were no chemicals added and many winemakers relied on the phases of the moon or its alignment with the sun or esoteric forces that bordered on superstitious. But only now are organic and biodynamic wines getting renewed attention.

Why? Let's examine the nature of these wines and how they are produced to understand why.

First, it should be noted that the use of the word *chemical* is often used for connoting unsafe, non-eco-friendly use not only in farming and winemaking but in our daily lives as our society forges towards a greener planet. But everything is a chemical. Yes, that may be a simplistic view, however, the main target of those "bad" chemicals is synthetic products that have been proven to be harmful to the environment. The use of chemicals in itself is not bad; we use them every day from brushing our teeth to treating illnesses. It is our growing knowledge of science that now allows us to make better and more informed decisions about what is good and what is not.

Organic wines are made using eco-friendly farming practices and "natural," environmentally safe products for growing grapes and making wine.

In the vineyard, organic growers forego the use of what some call "chemical poisons," namely synthetic chemical fertilizers, herbicides, insecticides and fungicides. Instead they rely on organic matter derived from sources on the property such as manure and processed grapes to provide nutrients from the soil to the vines. Vines are also trellised and trained and foliage is thinned, all to favor healthy grape growth and minimize the risk of rot, mildew or other vineyard diseases. Fertilizers, pesticides and the like are not allowed either. As an alternative, vineyards use cover crops such as plants and legumes to improve soil fertility and quality and reduce erosion and to promote a more balanced ecology to fight vine-damaging diseases, insects, and pests. The use of cover crops is a fundamental practice of sustainable agriculture.

In the winery, many "chemicals" are not allowed. These include yeast and bacterial cultures for alcoholic and malolactic fermentations (these can then only rely on indigenous yeast or bacteria found in the vineyard and winery), preservatives, synthetic fining agents as well as acids for increasing acidity. Some winemaking regions allow a very small amount of sulfite as a preservative but while others disallow it completely for wine to be certified organic. Perhaps this is the reason why organic wines have not caught on. Wine appreciation has been about aromas and flavors, but without sulfite, wine can quickly become devoid of some of those aromas and flavors. It is also less protected against oxidation and microbial spoilage with a much lesser aging potential and so enophiles have been disinterested. But with the move to healthier living, there is now renewed interest at least with new wine consumers. There is also evidence that organic grape juice contains higher levels of polyphenols including resveratrol which have demonstrated a high correlation with positive health attributes (see section *Wine and Health*).

Perhaps organic viticulture or organic agriculture in general, for that matter, can benefit from the work of the late agronomist Francis Chaboussou (1908–1985), a research scientist or more importantly, a plant pathologist with the National Institute of Agricultural Research (INRA) in France and author of *Healthy Crops: A New Agricultural Revolution*. Chaboussou's work and claims focus on the theory of trophobiosis which he supports with a meta-analysis of extensive scientific research, including his own, that spans half a century. José Lutzenberger (1926–2002), an agronomist and former Minister of the Environment in Brazil was a fervent advocate of the theory of trophobiosis and influenced agricultural practices in his native land.

Traditional viticulture currently practised at Tawse Winery, Ontario.
Courtesy of Fred Couch.

Dung-filled cow horns being prepared for eventual burial in the vineyard.
Courtesy of Montinore Estate.

Trophobiosis is derived from the Greek *trophikos* or nourishment, and *biosis* or mode of life. It defines the symbiotic relation where different organisms "cooperate" in return for nutrients or food. The scientific evidence is quite complex and to a large extent because of this complexity of interactions between soil, plants, parasites and their environment, it is still not well understood. The observations and conclusions, however, are quite compelling and make a very strong case for organic agriculture.

The theories purport that the use of artificial chemicals or what Lutzenberger calls "biocides," disrupt the plant's physiological balance. The strongest criticism though is in the use of insecticides which have been proven to have effects beyond the surface of crops; they in fact enter the plants via its structures (i.e., leaves, roots, trunk, etc.) and disrupt their metabolism including their ability to synthesize proteins. The plants weaken and become vulnerable to pests and diseases. Then, there is strong evidence that fighting a disease with pesticides only creates a vicious cycle. Plants develop resistance to the disease and then a new disease sets in and which requires a new pesticide. In viticulture specifically, Chaboussou makes a case against grafting by outlining evidence that supports that *vinifera* cultivars have been deficient since the post-phylloxera grafting onto American rootstocks. One such deficiency is chlorosis, a condition manifested as yellowing or blanching of leaves due to, for example, parasitic attacks or mineral deficiencies. Unfortunately, the work of Chaboussou is still relatively unknown at least in North America perhaps because his book was only translated into English in 2005, twenty years after first being published in French.

Sustainable winemaking shares many of the principles of organic agriculture and winemaking but the overarching goal is one of environmental stewardship—that is, it seeks to integrate best practices in the vineyard, in the winery, and in the community that are environmentally and socioeconomically responsible and self-perpetuating. For example, sustainable winemaking practices include:

carbon footprint reduction; how valuable resources such as water are being managed and how waste, including wastewater and pomace (the solid remains of grapes) are disposed of, or recycled as in the case of product packaging; and how pesticides and other agricultural or winemaking by-products are being managed. There are now best-practices and guidelines developed by industry leaders such as the Wine Institute and California Association of Winegrape Growers (CAWG) who formed the California Sustainable Winegrowing Alliance (CSWA) and by "green" third parties that also provide certification as an incentive to become sustainable. For example, wineries can obtain LEED (Leadership in Energy and Environmental Design) certification if their building design and winery operations comply with the "green building" criteria developed by the USGBC (U.S. Green Building Council). In Canada, the CaGBC has tailored USGBC criteria for "Canadian climates, construction practices and regulations."

Then there is biodynamic viticulture which takes organic farming several steps further—albeit in very different directions—and is based on the theories of Rudolf Steiner (1861–1925), an Austrian philosopher and esotericist who founded biodynamic agriculture in Germany in 1924. Many of his theories are not unlike those put forward by Robert B. Thomas in 1792 and published ever since in *The Old Farmer's Almanac* for forecasting weather and planning gardening activities. According to the almanac, weather forecasts are derived from a "secret formula" based on "three scientific disciplines to make [their] long-range predictions: solar science, the study of sunspots (which they define as magnetic storms on the surface of the Sun) and other solar activity, climatology, the study of prevailing weather patterns, and meteorology, the study of atmosphere."

The focus of biodynamic viticulture has been on farming practices because wine really *is* made in the vineyard, as the saying goes. Winemaking is non-interventionist and minimalist, reduced to necessary tasks only such as racking. Nicolas Joly (1945–), an outspoken current-day preacher of biodynamic viticulture describes the role of the winemaker as one of "midwifery" in *Biodynamic Wine Demystified*. Ouch!

As the word suggests and according to Joly, biodynamic deals with forces that energize life. Perhaps a more academic definition would be that biodynamic farming revolves around theories or doctrines of the interplay of planetary forces or cosmic forces, and how they affect living things, all synergistically cohabiting in perfect balance. Machines and all forms of modern technology including biochemical technology to fight vineyard malaises which disrupt this delicate balance are verboten.

Then a vineyard is simply seen as a holistic, self-perpetuating *energy management system* where the energy in the vine is modulated by the inherent energy of natural forces. For example, as the sun rises, it exerts an attraction force and "pulls up" the vine, and centripetal planetary forces "push" the roots down into the soil. Trying to irrigate the vine—with processed water and therefore its energy disrupted—would thus counter those forces and disturb the balance but rainwater has the right balance of energy.

Natural preparations are also used—again synergistically with other forms of life, namely animal organs—to enhance that energy. Most common are dung-filled cow horns buried in the vineyard before the winter. The horns are retrieved in the spring, mixed with natural water in very precise fashion to optimize energy, and then the mixture is sprayed over the vineyard at sunset so as to allow the force of the setting sun to draw down the mixture into the soil. But not any horns will do—only horns from lactating cows will work.

Sounds like a lot of cow manure? Not according to the fairly long list of Demeter-certified biodynamic viticulturists from France to New Zealand, including: Nicolas Joly's Clos de la Coulée de Serrant in the Loire Valley, Domaine Zind Humbrecht in Alsace with an unquestionable reputation, Domaine Leroy headed by Lalou Bize Leroy and formerly of Domaine Romanée-Conti (DRC) fame in

Burgundy, Alvaro Palacios in Spain, the Benziger Family Winery in California, Southbrook Vineyards in Niagara-on-the-Lake, Ontario, and Millton Vineyards in New Zealand, just to name a few. Anyone who has had the opportunity to taste their wines—and who could afford them—will concur with the superlative quality, individuality, and expression of the *terroir* of the wines.

Scientists may cringe at the unsubstantiated theories; after all, the essence of any science is proof through observation and experimentation to validate hypotheses. And so, although the theories of biodynamic farming cannot be scientifically proven, they cannot be disproved either; and Joly implores that we "liberate a large part of the scientific world from the cul-de-sac in which its materialistic dogmas have imprisoned it." Ouch again!

But I imagine that it will be a while longer before this pseudoscience gains acceptance with the masses and certainly not with wineries in the short term. Wineries are already faced with high capital outlays and small returns, often with breakeven periods of five, ten or more years. Asking them to endorse and implement biodynamic viticulture, where it can take ten to fifteen years to turn a vineyard around, simply would not fly. Their objective is to balance the books and that takes considerable energy, more than any cosmic force can impart.

∿

I am a home winemaker, and my (Italian) dad told me never to "disturb" wine on a full moon, otherwise, it will turn cloudy. Is there any truth to that myth?

AH YES! LEAVE IT TO THE OLDER-GENERATION Italian home winemakers to add a dash of their "scientific knowledge" to winemaking. Some of it borders on the paranormal. And last time I checked, none were familiar with the work of Rudolf Steiner.

As the son of an Italian immigrant, a home winemaker too (of course), the fall season in Montréal was exciting for me—exciting for many reasons but mainly because it was the start of winemaking season. I always enjoyed trekking to the local Italian market to buy what now seems like it was always *Alicante* (Alicante Bouschet) for red wine and *Moscato* (Muscat) or Thompson Seedless for white wine. There was something fun about buying grapes. Perhaps it was because I knew that it would soon be transformed by some kind of magic into wine after I developed blisters from working the hand-operated crusher. The fact that I did not know the chemistry—and neither did my father—made the whole experience intriguing. And of course we would have friends and family over, and that meant party, food and wine, well—soft-drinks for us younger ones. But I digress.

Once the wine started fermenting and then "self-stabilized"— this generation of Italian home winemakers was very non-interventionist—it would then need at least one or two rackings and soon be bottled for drinking. And I remember my dad warning me against disturbing, as in racking, wine on a full moon or on a cloudy or rainy day. He never did offer me a convincing explanation except to say that it would make the wine *turbido* or cloudy.

I thought, is this some kind of witchcraft? I did learn though that you should never, ever, double-guess this "scientific" principle.

Who knows? Maybe Steiner did align the planets and stars for my dad.

Only later in life as an avid winemaker myself did I decide to investigate this further, then armed with knowledge of chemistry, though "astropsychemistry" would have served better if such a science existed. At first it made sense. A full moon is closer to earth and causes greater atmospheric pressure that keeps dissolved gas— mainly, carbon dioxide, oxygen, and sulfur dioxide—in the wine; otherwise the gas under a low pressure would try to come out of solution and cause turbidity by agitating particles back into suspension. But then this theory did not support the effects of a cloudy or rainy day where atmospheric pressure is lower.

Based on my crude experiments, I could only conclude that there is no detectable difference between a wine processed during a full moon with one processed on a nice day. And now driven by financial and market pressures as a commercial winery operator, we never do worry about the weather or a full moon, that is unless we decide to take up biodynamic winemaking.

~

I have seen a gizmo that claims to "age" wine instantly to improve taste—all within thirty minutes—using some kind of magnet. Does it really work?

AH! THE LURE OF THE THERAPEUTIC magic of magnetic jewelry and all that is magnetic; and wine has not been spared of this malarkey.

Gimmicks that promise to "age" wine and improve taste have become popular. For as little as $34.95, the taste of wine can be made to improve while pouring as it traverses a magnetic field in split seconds. For a few dollars more, you can age a whole bottle in thirty minutes using a magnetic field that will turn a tannic wine into a velvety-soft, hedonistic one and shave off years of cellaring. (Why would anyone want to accelerate aging after we winemakers work so very hard to craft cellar-worthy wines?) And for a mere hundred dollars more, you can even eliminate red wine headaches, assuming you do not over-indulge, of course.

Unsubstantiated scientific claims of the effects of magnetic fields on wine range from the credible to the absurd. The only substance behind these claims is endorsements from consumers, people in various fields of the wine trade, and at least one Master of Wine, and from uncontrolled, unscientific experiments. To have any validity and credibility, scientific claims must be substantiated by scientific experiments, the results of which should go through a rigorous peer-review process—the most important part of the process.

Let's look at some specific, scientific claims that are making the rounds in product literature and on the Internet.

One claim is that:

A magnetic field creates a flux path that 1) bonds electrically-charged molecules and cause tannin molecules to *lengthen*, resulting in softer tannins, and that 2) aligns other components [presumably fruit esters], making the wine smell and taste fruitier. These are equivalent to years of cellaring.

Another claim that conflicts with the first, although the net effects on the wine are the same, is that the tannin molecules "are broken up or otherwise affected." This is not exactly what we could call a precise scientific explanation. The claim goes on to assert that the magnetic field "accelerates aeration because the magnetic field attracts the highly magnetic oxygen molecules." Yet another claim is that "the magnetic treatment can eliminate red wine headaches," supposedly because "the tannin molecules are broken up."

Does that mean that other molecules might be broken up into other components, potentially harmful ones, unbeknownst to a drinker? And if molecules can be broken up by a weak magnetic field, then why nothing happens to our bodies when subjected to the much stronger field used in MRI (magnetic resonance imaging) machines? But "magnetic oxygen molecules"—a claim probably drawing on the fact that elemental oxygen is strongly electronegative—must be the most absurd explanation.

The reality—scientifically speaking—is that magnets cannot effect such chemical changes; they can, however, effect physical changes but again not in wine and not the kinds claimed in these gizmos. There is nothing in wine that could cause a physical change. The reason why wine does in fact change as it ages is because of the very slow polyphenol polymerization and sedimentation; and we will focus on tannins because these are the target culprits in the claims.

Myth or fact: The cycle of the moon affects winemaking operations and wine quality?

The *Clef du Vin*® for "aging" wine on demand.

Tannins have a fining effect that causes precipitation when the negatively charged molecules bind to positively charged ones but the reaction is not affected by any magnetic field. Tannins also belong to the class of phenol compounds which are characterized by groups of benzene rings with hydroxyl groups (in its simplest form, you can think of phenol as a molecule of water with one hydrogen atom replaced by a benzene ring). As phenols oxidize and polymerize, complex phenolic polymers are formed which change the organoleptic qualities of the wine. Think of a cut apple browning as it sits on the kitchen counter. It is the same reaction. The oxidation and polymerization occur when dissolved oxygen (already in wine) reacts with the phenols. The rate of reaction depends on the wine's chemistry such as the amount of free sulfur dioxide and pH as well as environmental conditions such as cellaring temperature but not magnetic fields. And so, when a bottle is opened and wine is poured it aerates causing rapid phenolic oxidation and polymerization which change the characteristics of the wine. It is easy then to attribute the changes to some magnet unless you set up a proper experiment to determine any causal effects.

I did. My *subjects* whom I consider super tasters because they have extremely discerning palates and who were not given any information about the experiment or wines could not detect any significant changes between a wine and its *magnetized* version. The control wine poured straight from the bottle ranked slightly higher than the magnetized wine although most found them very similar. (A third sample decanted a couple of hours ahead ranked the least favorite with a score that was still quite different from the control. So much for decanting! See page 131.) And although I never had the chance to taste a wine at the North Pole and compare it to the same wine at the equator, where the magnetic field is only half as strong, I cannot find any scientific evidence purporting any magnetic effect.

So before you go out and buy such gizmos, consider the chemistry and the scientific evidence. Better yet, splurge the $34.95

on a fine bottle of ready-to-drink wine; it will surely give you greater pleasure though perhaps a small headache—but do not bother with the magnetic jewelry.

~

Speaking of gizmos, for my birthday I received a paddle-like gadget that promised to modify organoleptic qualities of wine in controlled fashion. Is this another gimmick?

THIS ONE IS QUITE INTERESTING and has some merit—again, scientifically speaking.

The device, the invention of French chemist and enologist Lorenzo Zanon and French sommelier Thomas Franck, consists of a stainless steel paddle incorporating a small alloy disc measuring approximately six millimeters (a quarter of an inch) that can be used to determine the aging potential of wine and, yes, modify organoleptic qualities such as softening tannins and developing aromas and flavors. The size and alloy have been precisely manufactured so that a one-second dip in 100 mL (about 3½ fl oz) of wine equals to one year of aging. The patent states that although the device does not age wine, the organoleptic effects are similar. But with the price ranging from $120 to $300—the most expensive version is a kit that includes one paddle for sampling wine in a glass, one for a bottle, and a pocket-sized version—this calls for some scientific sleuthing.

The claim is based on the fact that wine undergoes very slow bottle maturation or what enologists define as a transition from a reductive state to an oxidative one. As we have already seen, the rate of transition or aging depends on the chemistry of the wine, namely its redox potential and storage conditions. If storage conditions are assumed ideal and kept constant, the reaction between the wine and the alloy can be used to gauge the aging potential.

The alloy contains ninety-five percent copper, three percent gold, and two percent silver. These metals scavenge any free sulfur-containing compounds that are maintaining the wine in a reductive state, thereby causing the wine to move towards the oxidative state as metal sulfides form and free aromatic compounds. Aromatic alcohols, phenols and other aromatic compounds become slowly oxidized to give rise to different aromas and flavors. Depending on the redox state of the wine, the transformation can be positive or it can turn the wine into an unpleasant drink.

The use of copper is well known in treating sulfide-affected wines but not silver and gold.

You want to test the chemistry but do not want to invest hundreds of dollars? Not a problem; you can do it for a cent with a copper penny, i.e., a pre-1982 U.S. penny or a pre-1996 Canadian penny. Older penny coins contain ninety-five percent copper with the rest a mix of zinc and tin whereas newer pennies have a zinc or steel core with less than five percent copper plating. Just keep in mind that a penny is about twenty millimeters (three-quarters of an inch)—more than three times the size on the gadget—and so you will have to adjust your dip time accordingly to about a third of a second or increase the sample from 10 mL (a third of an ounce) to 33 mL (one ounce).

~

Wine and Health

~

THE USE OF WINE AND OUR STRONG convictions of its health benefits, abstainers and teetotalers notwithstanding, are probably as old as wine itself dating back to the first civilizations in the ancient world. In Mesopotamia ca. the third millennium BC, the Babylonians believed wine to have medicinal and therapeutic effects and it was considered so pure and free of contaminations that it was preferred—along with beer—over water. In Ancient Egypt more than two thousand years BC, wine also became a common ingredient in "prescription drugs" for curing a variety of ailments. The drugs were formulated using other ingredients too, such as water and particularly those derived from medicinal plants.

And stories abound from the Far East where the Chinese would lace wine with animal parts to concoct drugs to cure just about any ailment. Even Hippocrates, the father of medicine who had a keen sense of physiological and metabolic reactions in the human body not only used wine as a prescription drug in Ancient Greece but also pioneered it into an antiseptic for treating wounds.

The link between wine and its medicinal and therapeutic benefits grew stronger through the various eras and Middle Ages up to modern times. So compelling was the link that following the decreasing death rate of convicts and migrants who were treated with wine aboard Australia-bound ships in the early part of the nineteenth century, it spawned the founding of vineyards and wineries by British doctors throughout the rest of the century. Many such wineries have grown into global businesses responsible for some of the largest wine outputs in the world. For example, Lindemans and Penfolds were founded in the early 1840s by Drs. Henry J. Lindeman and Christopher R. Penfold, respectively.

But as wine became integral to religions from Biblical times and the evils of alcohol took root in societies, wine—its health benefits and sociological impacts—became very controversial and spawned the anti-alcohol temperance movement in colonial America. In 1916, federal health authorities removed alcohol from the *United States Pharmacopeia (USP)*, the authority responsible for implementing and managing standards for all prescription and over-the-counter medicines as well as health care products manufactured or sold in the United States. Then in 1920, the Volstead Act was enacted under the Eighteenth Amendment to the United States Constitution making the manufacture, sale, importation, and distribution of alcohol illegal which lasted until 1933 when the Twenty-first Amendment was ratified to repeal National Prohibition. During Prohibition, consumption of alcohol and homemade wine for personal use was still allowed though each state and often towns or counties were left to implement further control according to local needs. Wine for sacramental and medicinal uses was also exempt. In Canada, provinces had already started implementing prohibitory laws in 1917.

Much research on the health benefits of wine has been documented particularly since the nineteenth century. But the temperance movement had been strong and gained renewed momentum in the 1980s in advocating the evils of alcohol on public health. Mothers Against Drunk Driving (MADD), a now very influential organization, was first founded in 1980. Then during Ronald Reagan's first presidential term in the 1980s, First Lady Nancy Reagan launched the "Just Say No" drug awareness campaign which naturally included alcoholic beverages. Senator James Strom Thurmond, whose daughter was killed by a drunk driver in 1993 and whose wife later became addicted to alcohol, was a long-time, staunch anti-alcohol advocate. He led the offensive responsible for implementing (in 1988) the now-familiar warning on labels of all wines sold in the U.S. The ATF (Bureau of Alcohol, Tobacco, Firearms and Explosives, now the Alcohol and Tobacco Tax and Trade Bureau, or TTB) text reads as follows:

> GOVERNMENT WARNING: (1) According to the Surgeon General, women should not drink alcoholic beverages during pregnancy because of the risk of birth defects. (2) Consumption of alcoholic beverages impairs your ability to drive a car or operate machinery and may cause health problems.

But there was a major turnabout in 1991 when French scientist Dr. Serge Renaud made public his theory of the French Paradox which observed that the French suffer a relatively low incidence of coronary heart diseases (CHD), which is the major cause of death in industrialized countries, despite having a diet relatively rich in satur-ated fats found in, for example, eggs, dairy products and particularly cheese, and meat. Renaud's work catapulted sales of red wine in the U.S. and a renewed interest in the health benefits of wine when CBS aired its *French Paradox* TV segment on *60 Minutes* that same year. The French Paradox, the countless epidemiological studies and laboratory studies and experiments, such as those by renowned Kaiser-Permanente cardiologist Dr. Arthur Klatsky make a strong case in asserting the J- or U-shaped relationships between the consumption of alcohol and mortality rate. More specifically, these have demonstrated that moderate alcohol consumption resulted in a lower mortality rate compared to abstainers and tee-totalers or heavy alcohol drinkers. As well, moderate consumption has also been linked to a lower morbidity (disease) rate.

Moderate consumption is generally defined to represent 14 g of pure alcohol (ethanol) per day which can be obtained from 148 mL (5 fl oz) of twelve-percent-alcohol wine—careful with that "two glasses a day" guideline—or from 355 mL (12 fl oz) of five-percent-alcohol beer or from 44 mL (1½ fl oz) of forty-percent-alcohol spirit. And to enjoy and maximize the health benefits of moderate drinking, consumption must be daily and not averaged out by, for example, drinking seven times the recommended amount at one Saturday-evening party, and should be part of a balanced diet and healthy lifestyle including regular exercise.

As of 1999, wine destined for the U.S. market could then be labeled by TTB approval with a *directional* health-related statement directing consumers "to consult [their] family doctor about the health benefits of wine consumption" or to request the U.S. Department of Health and Human Services' (HHS) and Department of Agriculture's (USDA) published *Dietary Guidelines for Americans* "to learn the health effects of wine consumption." But Senator Thurmond and temperance advocates such as the Center for Science in the Public Interest (CSPI) and MADD struck again and effectively forced the TTB in 2003 to defeat directional statements on labels on the grounds that these were inherently misleading and confusing and gave the impression that the government endorsed the health benefits of alcohol consumption which encouraged consumers to imbibe further. After all, the whole premise of alcohol control is that wine as well as beer and distilled spirits have been considered intoxicating beverages and not medicines.

The wine industry with the support of such trade organizations as the Wine Institute and the American Vintners Association (AVA) lobbied the federal agencies for more substantive health-related claims and reached a compromise of sort. Henceforth, under the authority of the Federal Alcohol Administration Act (FAA Act), the new TTB regulations stipulated in part that:

A specific health claim on a label or in an advertisement is considered misleading unless the claim is truthful and adequately substantiated by scientific evidence; properly detailed and qualified with respect to the categories of individuals to whom the claim applies; adequately discloses the health risks associated with both moderate and heavier levels of alcohol consumption; and outlines the categories of individuals for whom any levels of alcohol consumption may cause health risks.

Such requirements have made it almost impossible to obtain approval to include health claims, directional or substantive, on labels or in advertisements particularly that claims must contain a disclaimer "advising consumers that the statement should not encourage consumption of alcohol for health reasons ..." According to Richard Mendelson in *From Darling to Demon: A Legal History of Wine in America*, not a single health claim has been approved by the TTB since the regulation came into effect.

But there is hope. There has been vast progress in the last decade on the health benefits of moderate wine consumption. Though we—except for anti-alcohol advocates—have been thirsty for more good news on the role of wine on our health, research is nonetheless far from conclusive given the often contradictory findings and the breadth of malaises, illnesses and diseases on which wine is believed to have effects. The list ranges from heart diseases, strokes, cancer, dementia, including Alzheimer's disease, type 2 diabetes, to arthritis and osteoporosis, and yes, even erectile dysfunction just to name a few. But a great deal of focus has naturally been on cardiovascular and neurodegenerative diseases.

In this section we will examine the science of the complex interactions between wine and health that are so near and dear to our hearts—literally.

Ok, so we have heard a lot about the French Paradox and the health benefits of moderate consumption of red wine. What is it in red wine that makes it healthy, and why not white wine or other alcoholic drinks for that matter?

EARLIER EPIDEMIOLOGICAL STUDIES suggested that alcohol—and therefore, wine, beer and spirits—was the compound responsible for claimed health benefits though its negative effects such as alcoholism and social impacts, cognitive developmental deficiencies, fetal alcohol syndrome (FAS), and increased risk of breast cancer in women are undisputed.

In moderate consumption, alcohol has been shown to increase the amount of tPA, or tissue Plasminogen Activator, a substance that catalyzes the conversion of plasminogen to plasmin, the major enzyme responsible for clot breakdown. And in the May 31, 2009 issue, *Wine Spectator* cites a Stanford University research which claims that aldehyde dehydrogenase-2 (ALDH2) enzymes process the alcohol and "eliminate toxic byproducts created by the break-down of fats in cells during a heart attack. Eliminating the byproducts prevents additional damage to the heart cells."

Although alcohol does play a favorable role, more recent studies have demonstrated that red wine provides further protection against illnesses and diseases and, therefore, that there are other important healthy compounds in red wine not found in white wine, beer or spirits. These healthy compounds belong to a class of compounds known as *polyphenols* of which there are two types in red wine: non-flavonoids and flavonoids. The word "flavonoid" is derived from the Latin *flavone*, meaning "yellow"—and not "flavor"—which tends to confuse people.

Nonflavonoids include stilbene polyphenols (also known as *stil-benoids*) such as resveratrol from grape pulp, and hydroxycinnamic and hydroxybenzoic acid derivatives such as gallotannins and ellagitannins found in oak-aged wines. Gallotannins and ellagitannins are better known as *hydrolyzable tannins* and are copolymers of gallic and ellagic acids and glucose, respectively.

Until recently, resveratrol (3,5,4'-trihydroxystilbene) was believed to be the main compound responsible for the health attributes in red wine. However, modern quantification methods reveal that the amount of resveratrol in wine is too low, particularly in wines processed with fining agents such as PVPP, to be of any important health consequence on its own. But a diet rich in resveratrol from fruit, vegetables, nuts, and wine has been linked, along with a healthy lifestyle, to longevity in humans according to Dr. Joseph Maroon, a world-renowned neurosurgeon and author of *The Longevity Factor*. He has extensively studied Dr. David Sinclair's research on the subject. Sinclair is Director of the Paul F. Glenn Laboratories for the Biological Mechanisms of Aging at Harvard Medical School and a prominent researcher on the biology of longevity. His team recently demonstrated in laboratory experiments that resveratrol has life-extending activity in not only normal mice but obese ones too by activating "survival" genes. It has also been demonstrated that resveratrol increases the production of nitric oxide (NO) by the endothelium (the thin layer of cells that line the interior surface of blood vessels). Endothelial nitric oxide is a vasodilator meaning it dilates arteries in our bodies to protect organs from ischemic damage.

It is interesting to note that resveratrol molecules are manufactured under stress in plants as a mean to fight off fungal infections. Then too, resveratrol is also classified as a phytoalexin (antibiotics produced by plants that are under attack) and, therefore, concentrations of resveratrol are highest in grapes grown in cool and wet climates. This is the basis of the *Xenohormesis Hypothesis* which states that "animals have evolved to sense stress signaling molecules in other species, in order to gain advance warning of a deteriorating environment." This was postulated by Sinclair and colleague Konrad Howitz and helps explain the French Paradox. Maroon also states that *V. rotundifolia* Muscadine grapes are uniquely beneficial because these possess an extra chromosome (compared to *V. vinifera* cultivars) that produces the phytochemical ellagic acid, and is then transformed into ellagitannins which are believed to provide anticancer and other health benefits.

Flavonoids are a group of compounds mainly found in grape skins, stems and seeds. Flavanols (also known as *flavan-3-ols*) such as catechin and epicatechin are flavonoids found abundantly in grape seeds (as well as other "health foods" such as green tea and dark chocolate) and are responsible for imparting that familiar astringency sensation from tannic wines. There are also anthocyanins such as delphinidin and malvidin which are responsible for the red color found in grape skins and subsequently imparted to red wine during maceration and fermentation. And there are flavonols such as quercetin which were found to be strong biological antioxidants providing a number of health benefits that are maximized in the presence of resveratrol which quercetin more readily absorbs.

Recent research, particularly that of Roger Corder, a professor of experimental therapeutics at the William Harvey Research Institute in London, England and author of *The Red Wine Diet*, now demonstrates that procyanidins are the active components.

Procyanidins, a subclass of flavanols is also known as *proanthocyanidins* or as *procyanidin oligomeric proanthocyanidins (OPC)* or as *condensed tannins* because they are formed from condensation of flavanols. They are found in great concentrations in grape seeds (which explains the recent grape seed oil rage) and consist of long chains of repeated units of other flavanols such as catechin and epicatechin. Young red wines are most rich in procyanidins and as wine ages, procyanidin molecules polymerize into longer, heavier and less soluble chains which then precipitate to the bottom of barrels, tanks or bottles. Logically it follows then, as Corder asserts, that the health benefits of red wine are maximized when drunk young. Moreover, different grapes contain different amounts of procyanidins and Corder's research singles out Tannat as the most procyanidin-rich red *vinifera* variety.

Tannat grapes are used to craft the wonderful wines of Madiran, an important appellation at the foothills of the Pyrénées Mountains in southwestern France, and of Uruguay in southeastern South America. Tannat-based wines are remarkably deep-colored, concentrated, and highly tannic as its name would suggest when vinified using traditional winemaking techniques that emphasize phenolic extraction and little or no fining and filtration. Red wines made using carbonic maceration or vinified as rosés or using a short maceration period will only contain low levels of procyanidins. As we have seen earlier, polyphenols are not as soluble in grape juice and become more soluble in wine as the alcohol content increases during fermentation.

Procyanidin concentration in grapes also depends on the age of the vines as well as viticultural practices. Stressing vines, for example, by limiting water intake and harvesting at low yields can be beneficial in this respect and the older the vines, the better owing to the additional stress of age which tends to favor phenolic concentration. A long, slow growing season is always preferred, however, we cannot control Mother Nature.

So how do procyanidins work in our bodies to reduce risks of atherosclerosis, cancer, dementia, diabetes and other malaises and diseases? There are various biological mechanisms two of which we examine here: antioxidant by reducing oxidative stress, and hypolipemic (as the name suggests—hypolipemic refers to a substance or compound that lowers the concentration of fats in the blood).

Procyanidins are potent biological antioxidants (so is resveratrol) much like vitamins C and E. They are capable of fighting free radicals responsible for aging and diseases. Free radicals are atoms, molecules or ions with unpaired electrons which makes them highly reactive and which can attack and damage key components in living cells, proteins within cells as well as DNA and can disrupt their proper functioning to initiate a disease such as CHD or malignant cancer. In her booklet *Resveratrol*, Matilde Parente, MD aptly likened the oxidative damage caused by free radicals to rust.

Procyanidins also inhibit LDL (low-density lipoprotein) cholesterol better known as *bad cholesterol*, and raising the level of HDL (high-density lipoprotein) cholesterol or the *good cholesterol*. LDL cholesterol is responsible for coronary thrombosis, i.e., platelet formation in blood clotting leading to LDL cholesterol oxidation and then to atherosclerosis—the most common form of arterio-sclerosis in which fatty deposits build up in arterial walls thereby restricting blood flow—and increasing the risk of myocardial infarction (heart attack). Saturated fats from red or processed meats and trans-fats are the major culprits of LDL cholesterol. Triglycerides, the main constituent of vegetable oil and animal fats are also implicated in atherosclerosis. HDL cholesterol contains more proteins and less fat and actually removes LDL cholesterol from blood and the lining of arteries and transports it to the liver for breakdown and excretion.

On the lighter side of things, NYDailyNews.com reports that women who drink two glasses of wine a day experience greater sexual satisfaction than non-drinkers or one-glass-a-day drinkers according to researchers from the University of Florence, Italy. We can safely extrapolate these results to men, without the need for any scientific studies. But gentlemen (and post-menopausal women), be forewarned—alcohol exacerbates snoring which your partner may find unromantic and be less inclined to invite you again for another sexual escapade. So go easy on the wine (and other alcohols, particularly distilled spirits) and stick to moderate consumption.

Need any more good news to make wine a part of your daily diet?

≈

My dietitian recommended that I avoid wine in trying to lose weight. Are wines that high in calories? Will I not lose out on those healthy polyphenols?

GENERALLY, THE RECOMMENDED DAILY calorie intake for women is 2,000 Calories and 2,500 for men though these will vary based on age, height and weight and body composition and level of daily activity. (Note: 1 Calorie is the same as 1 kilocalorie or 1,000 calories, and although *Calories* and *calories* are used interchangeably, the use of either usually means Calories.) The main sources of calories in wine are alcohol (ethanol) and sugar. Let's calculate the caloric intake of wine knowing that ethanol and pure sugar deliver approximately 7 and 4 Calories per gram, respectively.

Assuming a daily consumption of two glasses (150 mL, 5 fl oz) of dry, twelve-percent-alcohol (by weight) wine, total ethanol consumption is 14 g which delivers 98 Calories, and total sugar consumption (to be conservative, we assume a dry wine at 5 g/L of residual sugar) is 0.75 g, which delivers 3 Calories, for a grand total of 101 Calories, or about four to five percent of the recommended daily intake. Obviously, the more sugar the wine contains the more calories it delivers. Those two glasses of Sauternes (sweet white wine) with that luscious foie gras can easily deliver 225 Calories or more and that is just the wine. With seared foie gras, it could put you close to 1,000 Calories!

But, in any discussion around calories, we also need to consider carbohydrates (carbs)—those organic compounds consisting only of carbon, hydrogen, and oxygen with the general chemical formula $C_n(H_2O)_n$. The science of carbohydrates is quite complex but for all intents and purposes carbs are saccharides or sugars such as glucose, fructose, and sucrose. In wine, the primary sources of carbs are the *reducing sugars* which include residual (unferment*ed*) sugars, like, the six-carbon monosaccharides glucose and fructose, and unferment*able* sugars such as the five-carbon monosaccharide pentose.

So how many carbs are there in wine? There is no simple

calculation. It must be determined analytically using laboratory techniques. Generally, the range is 1–5 g of carbohydrates in those same two glasses (150 mL, 5 fl oz) of dry wine. As sweetness (residual sugar content) increases carbohydrates increase and can rise drastically for sweet dessert wines. The National Agricultural Library of the US Department of Agricultural has created a database accessible at http://www.nal.usda.gov/fnic/foodcomp/search/ which lists carbohydrates and other nutritional data for food and wine where you can also zero in on specific wine styles and varietals.

Certainly, those calorie and carb numbers seem high when we are trying to cut back but with a balanced diet and lifestyle and considering all the health-promoting compounds in red wine, why give wine a pass? Alternatively, look for procyanidin-rich food as well as dealcoholized (red) wine. Yes, dealcoholized wine still contains high levels of procyanidins. And try and cut back on all those other calories and carbs that do not deliver healthy nutrients.

~

I have heard all sorts of contradictory information about sulfites, headaches after drinking red wine, and allergies. I cannot make heads or tails of this. Can you explain?

THOSE BAD SULFITES; THEY ARE such an easy target. What else can people blame for headaches after drinking red wine? After all, there is even a regulation for all wines containing more than 10 ppm of sulfites sold in the U.S. that requires the mandatory mention CON-TAINS SULFITES on labels—again, courtesy of Senator Strom Thurmond. So there must be some health concerns with sulfites.

But why is that not indicated on other sulfite-containing food and beverages?

Why is wine singled out?

All are valid, interesting questions.

Recent research has shed some light on this controversy as only a very small segment of the population—approximately one percent—is actually allergic, exhibiting asthmatic reactions, but not experiencing headaches. In fact, very few people if any actually complain of headaches after drinking white wines which typically contain higher levels of sulfite as these are more prone to spoilage and therefore need added protection.

So why are people getting a headache after moderate drinking of red wine?

The answer lays in biogenic amines, namely histamine and tyramine both of which are known to have physiological effects. Those individuals that have the digestive enzymes (amine oxidases) to inactivate the biogenic amines will not suffer any ill effects but for others the amines can spell a head-splitting ache or migraine.

Histamine is derived from the amino acid histidine and is believed to cause headaches with some doctors recommending taking antihistamine tablets before drinking red wine if one is susceptible. Tyramine is derived from tyrosine and is believed to trigger migraines. Both amines are produced in only very tiny amounts in wine but their effects are exacerbated in the presence of alcohol. And reds usually have higher levels of alcohol than whites and, therefore, headaches are more common after drinking red wine.

Where do histamine and tyramine come from?

Both are by-products of malolactic fermentation—a wine-making technique mostly used in red wine production—where lactic acid bacteria convert malic acid into lactic acid. But only some types of bacteria produce the amines and, therefore, only those red wines affected by histamine or tyramine-producing bacteria will contain the effecting amines.

How can we—the consumers—tell?

We cannot.

As for asthmatic attacks, sulfur dioxide causes inflammation of mastocytes or mast cells that reside in tissues including those in the lungs. The mast cells contain many granules rich in histamine and are released during the inflammation triggering the attack. For non-asthmatics, sulfur dioxide is considered safe when within prescribed legal limits. In fact, our body manufactures a small amount of sulfur dioxide during the metabolism of amino acids and converts it into harmless sulfate.

Are there sulfite-free wines?

No.

Sulfite, or more precisely, sulfur dioxide is a natural by-product of fermentation, albeit, in small quantities and, therefore, wine can never be totally free of sulfite unless DNA and genetic engineering research and development find a way to alter or remove the gene that codes for sulfite production.

And what about switching to organic wines?

Sure, they have much less sulfite but recent studies have shown a higher level of biogenic amines in organic wines than their non-organic counterparts.

Are you getting a headache yet?

⁓

I think I have been drinking a little too much wine at the party. Can I drink coffee to reduce the ill effects and fool the breathalyzer if I get pulled over by the police?

No.

Drinking and driving is without a doubt a recipe for trouble and trying to fool detection is both irresponsible and futile. Now that we have cleared our collective social conscience, let's look at the biochemistry and chemistry of alcohol to see why consumption and detection cannot be fooled.

Alcohol refers to a general class of organic compounds, and ethanol also known as *ethyl alcohol* is the specific type found in beer, wine and spirits. After ingestion, ethyl alcohol diffuses through the gut and into the bloodstream and to various organs including the liver. Diffusion into the bloodstream happens fairly quickly—on average in about one hour. Alcohol dehydrogenase (ADH) enzymes in the liver metabolize ethyl alcohol which is then oxidized to acetaldehyde, the actual compound that impairs our senses. Acetaldehyde is further oxidized by a molybdenum-containing enzyme, aldehyde dehydrogenase (ALDH), into acetic acid—the acid found in vinegar—which can cause liver damage until the acetaldehyde is fully oxidized and produces carbon dioxide and water. The carbon dioxide gas is exhaled through the lungs. The duration of this metabolic reaction varies based on an individual's weight, body fat, sex, race, drinking pattern and metabolism; for example, a 68-kilogram (150-pound) moderate-drinking male requires, on average, about one hour to metabolize a 150-mL (5-fl oz) glass of twelve-percent alcohol wine.

And why do Japanese generally have lower tolerance to alcohol? Because they have lower levels of molybdenum-containing enzymes.

Although there are various types of devices using different technologies, law enforcement use the Breathalyzer test to determine if an individual is intoxicated by measuring the person's Blood Alcohol Concentration (BAC) as a percentage of mass of ethyl alcohol by volume of blood. In much of Canada and the U.S., the legal limit of intoxication and driving impairment is 0.08 percent. Some countries have lower limits, for example, 0.05 percent resulting in a driving suspension of short duration compared to a DUI while others have zero tolerance. The test involves blowing air into an apparatus that contains an orange potassium dichromate solution. The device also contains sulfuric acid to collect alcohol as a solution. Ethyl alcohol in the exhaled air reacts with the solution and is oxidized to acetic acid and produces chromium sulfate causing the solution to turn shades of green and provide an estimate of BAC.

So drinking coffee cannot fool the Breathalyzer nor can breath mints or mouthwash. These can temporarily mask the smell but they do not affect BAC.

Yes, the test and device have known sources of errors but why risk it? So remember the chemistry and do not drink and drive.

~

I have been using "plastic" carboys in my winemaking, but I have recently heard that some types of plastic materials contain toxic substances. What should I do?

FOR MANY YEARS SODA-LIME (soft) glass carboys were the only practical containers for fermenting and aging that were available to home winemakers. However, these glass carboys are heavy, slippery when wet, and fragile—even when new. Micro cracks which develop in the surface of soft glass when it is exposed to caustic detergents, sanitizers and even water also make soft-glass carboys more fragile with use and time. Much wine has been spilled and many people have been injured as the result of accidental breakage. Light-weight, colorless, clear and durable PET (polyethylene tere-phthalate copolymer) fermentation and aging carboys and fittings were introduced around the turn of the century and have essentially replaced soft-glass carboys for home winemaking.

In sharp contrast to other types of plastic carboys, PET carboys do not scalp (release, pick up, or transfer) flavors into wines, can be specially manufactured to have negligibly low permeability for oxygen, are hydrophobic, therefore, making them easier to wash than glass, and are not damaged or stained by the washing and sanitizing agents commonly used in winemaking. Most plastics are not suitable for winemaking. Firstly, they are too permeable to oxygen. Secondly, they release chemicals some of which are considered toxic and some of which contribute off flavors. Thirdly, they absorb substances during washing, sanitizing and fermenting that can transfer into the next batch of wine. And lastly, they cannot withstand the chemicals in wines or those used in winemaking.

It is tempting to simply dismiss concerns about toxic substances because PET carboys (recycle number 1) are extremely safe, however, there is so much misinformation swirling about that some background is essential in order to separate fact from fallacy.

The most notorious of the chemicals released by plastics is bisphenol-A (BPA), a chemical that was first synthesized in 1891 and used as a nonsteroidal estrogen replacement hormone in the 1930s. Over the years, BPA has become increasingly important as a component in a wide variety of materials and today it is found in an incredibly diverse range of products—everything from dental sealants to the linings of food and beverage cans (including those for infant formulas) to PVC water pipes, to bottles and carboys, to cash-register receipts and on and on. At least seven billion pounds of BPA are produced annually and there is great industry resistance to regulating and restricting its use despite mounting evidence that virtually everyone is contaminated with sufficient concentrations of BPA to have some health impact. BPA has been linked to reproductive abnormalities, cancer, diabetes and heart disease. Polycarbonate (PC) bottles and carboys—which are marked with a recycle number of 7—are essentially pure, polymerized BPA. They also make poor winemaking carboys for many of the other reasons outlined above. BPA is not used to make PET plastics nor is it used as a starting material to make any of the materials used in the manufacture of PET.

Plasticizers for plastics are additives that give hard plastics such as polyvinyl chloride (PVC or vinyl) the desired flexibility and durability necessary to make them into products like carboys and tubing. Ortho-phthalate plasticizers such as di(2-ethylhexyl) phthalate (DEHP) and dibutyl phthalate (DBP) and the adipate plasticizer di(2-ethylhexyl) adipate (DEHA) have been associated with a variety of health problems, most notably reproductive abnormalities, abnormal fetal development, cancer and neurological disorders. At this point, it is important to underscore the fact that small differences in the way chemical molecules are assembled, even though they contain exactly the same numbers and types of atoms can make a huge difference in how they react. There have been and continue to be numerous instances on the Internet and in mainstream media, radio, TV and print where writers have lumped classes of chemicals together or mistaken one chemical for another because the names were similar. Therefore, *ortho-phthalate* plasticizers are frequently confused with the *tere-phthalate* monomer in PET. There is no need to add plasticizers to the PET copolymers used to make carboys because these PET copolymers have excellent characteristics without plasticizers. There is no reason to believe that DEHP, DBP, DEHA or other plasticizers will leach from PET carboys when the carboys are frozen, warmed, exposed to sunlight, washed and re-used or stored for long periods.

Another concern that is making the rounds in the media and on the Internet is antimony (abbreviated Sb) content in PET containers. Antimony is a heavy, silver white metal with many applications, predominantly in semiconductor manufacturing and as a hardener in lead for storage batteries. But antimony is used in a tri-oxide form, i.e., antimony (III) oxide, as a catalyst to speed the production of many types of PET. Antimony *trioxide* is not the same as antimony *metal*; the trioxide is very insoluble and is not considered especially toxic. It is also important to maintain perspective in relation to the concentrations involved. Catalysts function at minute concentrations relative to the volume of product they catalyze; only traces of antimony trioxide are present in PET. Of the traces of antimony trioxide present in PET, only traces of those traces might be expected to migrate into wine. In the final analysis, the amounts are on the order of parts per trillion (ppt). In terms of perspective, one ppt is the equivalent of 1 second in about 32,000 years. According to Health Canada, an adult takes in on average approximately 7.44 micrograms (a microgram represents one millionth of a gram) of antimony each day from all sources and about thirty-eight percent of this intake is expected to come from the consumption of water, typically municipal supplies. The few trillionths of a gram that using a PET carboy might contribute (compared to millionths ingested daily, i.e., a millionth less) to this total represents an amount so small as to be essentially negligible.

We can conclude that PET carboys and fittings are among the safest items we use in our daily lives. PET is also one of the most attractive plastics from the standpoint of recycling and the environment, especially when products made from it can be used again and again. In fact, some wineries are switching to snazzy-looking PET bottles to take advantage of the environmental benefits, cost efficiencies and market appeal.

~

How is it possible that winemakers die from exposure to carbon dioxide?

CARBON DIOXIDE IS A COLORLESS, odorless gas and a by-product of respiration in humans and animals—the result of glucose oxidation in a series of metabolic reactions in the body. Carbon dioxide is integral to biological lifecycles in small concentrations, however, it becomes an asphyxiant in concentrations exceeding ten percent. Vast amounts of the gas are produced in the huge stainless steel tanks used during alcoholic fermentation. The gas is vented to the outdoors but carbon dioxide is also approximately fifty percent heavier than air and has a tendency to sink to low levels and go unnoticed because it cannot be detected. When winery personnel enter these huge tanks to clean them out after fermentation and after grape solids have been removed there is still residual carbon dioxide surreptitiously present at deadly concentrations.

Winery personnel suffocating while cleaning tanks was unfortunately a regular occurrence until the 1960s when wineries started implementing proper ventilation and test protocols, but it still happens at wineries that fail to follow, or have not implemented, the protocols. It unfortunately happened as recently as in November 2008 when two amateur French winemakers suffocated in a poorly ventilated area while lending a helping hand to a winery friend.

~

Does air pollution and acid rain affect vines, grapes, and wine quality and ultimately my health? What about pesticides?

SPECIFIC POLLUTANTS OR CLASSES of pollutants are well known to have damaging effects on the environment such as ozone (triatomic oxygen) depletion and global warming and on our health when contaminants are beyond acceptable levels. Vineyards are typically situated in areas with low levels of pollution and are not of major concern. This does not mean that pollution should be ignored, however, there has been limited research on the impact of pollution on vineyards. It is a very complex area of research.

Let's examine the chemistry of pollutants and their impact on vine-growing specifically.

The earth's atmosphere comprises a number of gases mainly diatomic nitrogen and oxygen as well as carbon dioxide and water vapor. Every second of every day anthropogenic pollutants from car emissions, landfills and industrial processes are released into the atmosphere and react with its constituents. The major pollutants are sulfur oxides, carbon dioxide, nitrogen oxides, chlorofluoro-carbons (CFCs). When these gases reach the atmosphere they react with sunlight and atmospheric (diatomic) oxygen to form harmful substances.

Sulfur dioxide is known to have damaging effects to plants when in high concentrations; it is the result of oxidation of elemental sulfur such as in coal-burning processes. It also reacts with atmospheric oxygen to form sulfur trioxide, which then reacts with water vapor to form sulfuric acid in acid rain. A second component of acid rain is carbonic acid which is formed in a similar reaction from emitted carbon dioxide. But the most damaging component is hydrofluoric acid, formed from hydrogen fluoride, released from smelter operations and phosphorous fertilizer production, and water vapor in the atmosphere. When acid rain reaches the soil in vineyards, it lowers the pH, thereby, throwing soil chemistry off-balance making it difficult to grow premium grapes. Some of these acids are particularly corrosive and toxic and detrimental to vine growing.

Nitrogen oxide is found in car exhaust gas and is the result of the high-heat combustion of (diatomic) nitrogen. In the atmosphere, nitrogen oxide reacts with molecular oxygen to form nitrogen dioxide, the reddish-brown gas responsible for smog. Nitrogen dioxide is then photochemically converted back to nitrogen oxide along with an oxygen atom. The oxygen radical then reacts with molecular oxygen to form ozone in the lower atmosphere. Ozone is a strong irritant and is damaging to vines and crops.

Car exhaust also releases hydrocarbons that react with nitrogen oxide to form peroxyacetyl nitrate, a compound belonging to the class of peroxyacyl nitrates (PAN). PANs are powerful toxi-irritants present in photochemical smog that cause ozone to accumulate and are also highly damaging to vine physiology resulting in reduced yields. And until leaded (tetraethyl lead) gasoline was phased out, wines produced from vineyards located in close proximity to high-traffic roadways demonstrated higher levels of lead, a potent neuro-toxin responsible for lead poisoning. If lead enters the bloodstream, it can interfere with and disable delta-aminolevulinic acid dehydra-tase (ALAD) enzymes responsible for making hemoglobin. Hemo-globin is the iron-containing protein pigment occurring in red blood cells of vertebrates and functioning primarily in the transport of oxygen from the lungs to body tissues. Lead poisoning can then cause irreversible neurological damage as well as abdominal pain, gastro-intestinal problems, headaches, anemia, reproductive problems, and a multitude of other effects.

Chlorofluorocarbons (CFCs) belong to the class of haloalkanes.

They comprise alkanes such as methane or ethane with halogens such as chlorine or fluorine—and are well known to have harmful effects associated with ozone depletion. The halogen in CFCs reacts with ozone to form an oxide of the halogen plus molecular oxygen.

As for pesticides, it has been clearly proven that, environmental impacts notwithstanding, there are negligible residues in wine. Of course this assumes that pesticides are properly applied and well within the recommended treatment period prior to harvest. The various winemaking processes, namely crushing, pressing, fermentation, fining, filtration and aging cause the pesticide residues to disappear.

And what about the thick and heavy smoke from the devastating wildfires of the summer of 2008 that blanketed Northern California wine country? Some red wines from such hard-hit areas as Mendocino County have a decidedly smoky, charred aromas and burnt-wood, ashy tastes. The compounds responsible for smoke taint are guaiacol and 4-methylguaiacol, volatile phenols which are absorbed into grape skins—especially in thin-skinned varieties, such as Pinot Noir—and then extracted during maceration and exacerbated by fermentation. Whites are mainly spared since there is no skin maceration with the juice. Much research has been carried out on smoke-tainted wines in Australia where in 2003, smoke from wildfires also greatly affected vineyards. Using reverse osmosis and nanofiltration technologies the Australians have been able to reduce the culprit compounds down to non-detectable levels. VA Filtration (VAF), a company specializing in such services as removal of volatile acidity (VA), Brett (yeast infection), and TCA (corked wine) claims that they can now eliminate up to ninety-nine percent of the targeted sensorial characteristics by treating affected wine with a food-grade resin developed in Germany. Interestingly, if not puzzling VAF's website states that the "offensive compound(s) being removed are still not [known]."

But the astute reader will remember that guaiacol and 4-methylguaiacol are compounds found in toasted oak-aged wines where they are highly desirable.

It is quite the dichotomy!

∼

How was wine responsible for the development of Coca-Cola?

THE LINK IS COCAINE.

In 1863, Corsican chemist Angelo Mariani (1838–1914) developed *Vin Mariani*, a coca wine that had stimulating effects and used to treat morphine addiction and which was used as a "medicinal" beverage by the rich or famous from royalty and a U.S. President to Popes. Pope Leo XIII even awarded the wine a gold medal in recognition of its benefits. Its use was specifically exempted under National Prohibition in the U.S., as were other wine tonics for "treating" various ailments.

The special concoction was prepared by macerating *Erythroxylum coca* plant leaves in red wine to allow ethanol to extract cocaine. When ingested together, the liver metabolizes cocaine and ethanol into cocaethylene, a psychoactive ethyl homologue of cocaine and a potent drug that causes euphoric stimulation greater than cocaine alone.

Then in 1886, John Pemberton (1831–1888), a pharmacist in Atlanta, became fond of coca wine and created his own *French Wine Coca* which became very popular with American consumers. Because of the temperance movement and legislations in Atlanta in other Georgian counties, Pemberton had to develop a non-alcoholic version of his coca wine. That is when he introduced sugar syrup in his formula along with kola nuts into carbonated water and created *Coca-Cola*. But in 1906 as cocaine became a controlled substance because of its dangerous and addictive physiological effects, cocaine could no longer be used and was removed from the list of ingredients.

Considering current-day problems in North America associated with obesity such as elevated heart disease risks and type 2 diabetes, perhaps sugar should become a controlled substance and red wine promoted as invigorating beverage part of a healthy lifestyle.

∿

What do chocolate, Champagne and oysters have in common?

THIS IS AN INTERESTING question, particularly in the context of wine and health. Health, you ask? A healthy libido is a sign of, well, good health.

That's right! Chocolate, Champagne and oysters share the common belief of possessing aphrodisiac qualities. But unfortunately, all this aphrodisiac hogwash is just a myth.

Speaking of sexual desires and all: About enjoying that bottle of Champagne in a hot tub—it sounds very romantic, but it can be deadly. The high heat of water and the surrounding vapor increases body temperature and dilates blood vessels which cause the heart to work harder to pump blood throughout the body and if you mix in alcohol the effects become compounded. Sparkling wine accelerates this physiological process as the bubbles (in the wine, not the water) increases the rate of diffusion of alcohol into the bloodstream. Body temperature and blood vessel dilation can increase to levels that can trigger drowsiness or loss of consciousness which can cause drowning or quite possibly a stroke or heart attack. So save the bubbly until after the hot tub and after letting your body return to normal temperature.

∿

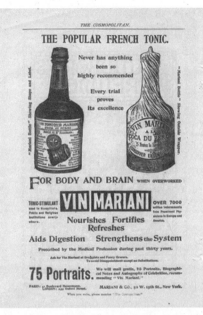

Late 19th century ad in *The Cosmopolitan* extolling the virtues
of *Vin Mariani*.

Many believe Champagne, oysters and chocolate to be aphrodisiacs.

What are ethyl carbamate and ochratoxin A, and why are wines tested for these substances?

ETHYL CARBAMATE (EC)—also known as *urethane*—is an ester of carbamic acid found in fermented food and beverages. In wine, it is a post-fermentation by-product measurable in trace amounts (in the μg/L, or ppb, range), and is the result of a reaction between ethanol and any compound that contains a carbamoyl (the radical NH_2CO- of carbamic acid) group such as urea or carbamoyl phosphate. Urea is produced during fermentation when yeasts metabolize α-amino acids—those amino acids characterized by a corkscrew shape and held into place by hydrogen bonds—such as arginine and citrulline (an arginine derivative). Urea can be minimized through the addition of DAP (diammonium phosphate) to consume nitrogen away from the amino acids, as well as choosing a yeast strain known to minimize EC production. Red wines have higher concentrations of such α-amino acids, particularly those with a high population of citrulline-producing lactic acid bacteria used for malolactic fermentation and, therefore, tend to have higher levels of EC.

Ethyl carbamate is believed to be a human carcinogen (and proven in animals), and for this reason, it is a closely monitored compound with strict permissible limits. For example, the maximum set under Health Canada's Contaminant Standards is 30 μg/L for table wines while the U.S. has set a voluntary limit of 15 μg/L. Limits for fortified (sweet) wines and distilled spirits are higher. It can be as high as 400 μg/L in fruit brandies and liqueurs. In fortified wines, a distilled spirit is added to stop the fermentation and causes a higher residual concentration of urea which would normally subdue if the fermentation was allowed to progress to dryness. In distilled spirits, the concentration is yet higher because the heating process catalyzes urea formation.

As for ochratoxin A according to *The Merck Index,* it is "reasonably anticipated to be a human carcinogen"—or mycotoxin, i.e., a toxic substance produced by a fungus and especially a mold—and a concern not only in wine but in other food and beverages including cereal products, dried fruits, and coffee. It is "reasonably" anticipated to be carcinogenic because of the limited experimental data from testing on animals; there are no comprehensive human studies that clearly demonstrate cause and effect.

Given the breadth of products that can become contaminated and the possible health implications on humans, ochratoxin A is now monitored by some governmental food inspection agencies or quality control boards who have set maximum allowable concentrations for specific kinds of food and beverages.

In Canada and the EU (the U.S. has not yet set regulatory limits) the maximum allowable in wine is 2 µg/L where molds from *Aspergillus* species, notably *A. carbonarius* and *A. ochraceus* as well as some species of *Penicillium* are known to produce ochratoxin A. The conditions for these molds to grow are not yet understood though it is believed that they require moisture and warm temperatures.

There is nothing different done in viticulture or winemaking that have caused this potential, albeit very, very small health concern; it is simply that our scientific knowledge has grown and laboratory techniques have been developed to track this naturally occurring mycotoxin. The challenge though is that current techniques cannot precisely quantify ochratoxin A concentration; in fact, measurements are based on the concentrations of other metabolites that accompany the production of ochratoxin A and carry an accuracy of only 0.5 µg/L.

So should ethyl carbamate and ochratoxin A be causes of concern to wine drinkers, particularly in light of recent studies extolling the health benefits of moderate red wine drinking? Certainly not. As with anything, dosage is what is important, and the miniscule amounts in wine are believed to pose no health risks.

$\backsim$

Wine Frauds

～

THE LURE OF EASY MONEY has not escaped the wine world where turning wine into profits is an elusive goal. There is an adage in the industry that says, "To make a small fortune in the wine business, you must start with a big fortune." How true!

And so it is that unscrupulous "business" people resort to adulteration and other tricks to increase sales and generate more profits. There have been many attempts to "cut" (dilute) wine with water to increase output, a practice known as *mouillage* in French, to add flavorings or even toxic substances to increase mouthfeel, aromas or "quality," or to use grape varieties of lesser quality instead of a premium variety declared on the label. In a scandal unearthed in 2008, E.&J. Gallo Winery had purchased more than thirteen million liters (3.5 million gallons) of "Pinot Noir" for their *Red Bicyclette* label from a Languedoc (France) wine merchant. French authorities convicted the cheaters with what amounted to a slap on the hand given the magnitude of the scam.

The high-end wine market has not been spared. So-called collector wines, highly sought for their high resale value, not for drinking pleasure, can fetch dizzying prices at auctions. In the heyday of the tech boom, the fine wine market grew at an unprecedented pace particularly in non-traditional Asian markets. These factors combined to spawn a counterfeit industry. There were those who bottled cheap wine under the guise of a premium label and some who even forged labels. It was big business. It was so big in fact, that auction houses and collectors had to go through great lengths to authenticate the origin—or what is called *provenance* in wine-speak—of highly praised bottles. Great strides have been made in analytical and laboratory methods to help establish provenance and authenticity, some of which are routinely used by regulatory bodies to control wine production and sales in their appellations. Protecting appellations is serious business.

Consider the latest black eye suffered by the Italian wine industry and the scandal involving premium Brunello wines from the 2003 to 2007 vintages from a handful of top estates in the DOCG (*Denominazione di Origine Controllata e Garantita*) appellation of Montalcino in Tuscany. DOCG regulations stipulate that Brunello di Montalcino and Rosso di Montalcino wines be produced strictly from one hundred percent Sangiovese grapes. Those estates' Brunellos and Rossos were found to contravene this regulation as they contained other varieties. Whole productions were impounded until the investigation would complete or were simply declassified to a lower appellation that allows other varieties to be blended though these would sell at much lower prices.

Here, we review some specific cases of fraudulence, some of which became international public-relations nightmares for those trying to protect their long-established image of world-class wine producers and the role wine science played in the ensuing investigations.

What scandal rocked the Austrian winemaking industry and tarnished their wines' reputation in the 1980s?

IN 1985 IN THE SMALL BUT wine-reputed city of Rust in Burgenland, during a difficult period in wine production and sales in Austria, some winemakers and wine merchants colluded to add antifreeze to wine to increase sweetness and to be able to charge a higher price. According to a *New York Times* report, the individuals involved acted on the devious advice of a consulting chemist who masterminded the alchemy. Antifreeze, they were told, would not be easily detected whereas added sugar would be—which is against wine regulations in Austria—although it could have been possible using gas chromatography–mass spectrometry (GC–MS) analytical methods. But it was not chemistry that alerted the authorities. Nope! The adulteration of millions of liters of wine and the ensuing scandal came to light when one of the unscrupulous co-conspirators filed a tax credit claim for his expense of antifreeze which was not on the list of approved wine additives. Winemaking laws in Austria have since been seriously tightened.

Antifreeze-laced wine was even referenced in the satirical *The Crepes of Wrath* TV episode of the *Simpsons* where, while boarding with a pair of crooks in a vineyard in France on a student exchange program, Bart was told to drink a glass of adulterated wine and that it would be good for him. The villainous winemakers had added antifreeze which they claimed is poison but when added in the right amount can do miracles and it would "add body" (though the writers translated the French *corps* to "kick") to the wine. But one crook exclaimed to the other that he added too much and that it may kill someone. The other swindler—obviously not familiar with Paracelsus' phrase that *the dose makes the poison*— replied, "Kill someone? Don't be ridiculous." They then proceeded to get Bart to drink the concoction to see if it would make him blind. Well, Bart did not go blind, and as he was later reporting his episode to a policeman, the latter exclaimed, "Antifreeze in the wine? That is a very serious crime." It is indeed a very serious crime, one with potentially deadly consequences.

Although the references are often to automobile antifreeze, the actual chemical added was diethylene glycol which is a by-product of antifreeze production and which has a very long history in food and beverage adulteration. Antifreeze consists of ethylene glycol, the simplest of the glycols or dihydroxy alcohols and is much more toxic than the diethylene form.

Both ethylene glycol and diethylene glycol belong to a class of alcohols called *diols* which contain two alcohol groups in their molecular structures. Both are odorless, colorless but syrupy and sweet-tasting making them an attractive drink for the unsuspecting, particularly children and pets, many of which have paid dearly after ingesting antifreeze from dripping cars in driveways or on the street. When ingested, ethylene glycol is metabolized by enzymes to produce an intermediary by-product that then oxidizes to glycolic acid (hydroxyacetic acid) and cause acidosis, a condition of decreased alkalinity of the blood resulting in symptoms such as nausea and vomiting. Glycolic acid then metabolizes into glyoxylic acid followed by oxalic acid, a strong dicarboxylic acid that can combine with calcium ions to form insoluble calcium oxalate salt deposits (kidney stones) in the kidneys leading to kidney failure and quite possibly death if the amount of calcium is reduced to a critically low level in the blood.

Although antifreeze is used jokingly in wine fraud discussions, it is clearly no laughing matter—it can be deadly. And yes, those two French crooks in the *Simpsons* were jailed … for "participating in a student exchange program."

~

What scandal crippled Italian wine exports in the 1980s?

THIS STORY UNFOLDS IN 1986 in the small commune of Narzole in the northwestern Italian province of Cuneo in the Piedmont region when again, in a similar incident to the Austrian scandal, some unscrupulous, chemistry-challenged father-and-son winemaking team added methanol to wine to boost their wine's alcoholic strength. After all, methanol (methyl alcohol) is alcohol but it can be easily confused with ethanol (ethyl alcohol). Surely two substances with only a small typographical change must be very similar. The names are very similar but the chemistry of the compounds is dramatically different—you can drink ethanol whereas methanol can actually kill you. A couple of dozen people did die and many more suffered illnesses in this scandal. The ensuing investigation determined that the wine contained almost twenty times the legal limit of methanol.

Alcohols are organic compounds made up of one or more hydrocarbons plus a hydroxyl group in their molecular structures.

Methanol is also known as *wood alcohol* and is a simple but highly toxic alcohol found in solvents and paint removers. It is also found in nontoxic concentrations in wine in the order of five to ten times less than regulatory limits. Methanol consists of a methyl (CH_3-) group as the only hydrocarbon attached to the hydroxyl group and is the result of the pectinolytic enzyme methylesterase breaking down the methoxyl $(-OCH_3)$ group in naturally occurring pectin in grape juice. If methanol is ingested, it oxidizes to formic acid and formaldehyde (formic aldehyde), also known as *methanal*, a very reactive aldehyde that can cause headaches, blindness or even death. Aldehydes are organic compounds containing a carbonyl group which consists of a carbon atom with a double bond to an oxygen atom.

Ethanol is a somewhat more complex alcohol and is the kind found in alcoholic drinks. Its molecular structure has an additional hydrocarbon branch consisting of one carbon and two hydrogen atoms which gives ethanol completely different characteristics. When it oxidizes, it forms acetaldehyde which is another aldehyde, however, this one is not toxic. Acetaldehyde is actually quite common in wines that have oxidized prematurely or when a partial bottle is left open for several days. The smell is unmistakable. Oxidized wine will take on a nut-like smell akin to Sherry wine. Ethanol oxidation to acetaldehyde is the chemical reaction that Breathalyzer tests rely on to measure blood alcohol levels (BAC).

Perhaps these winemakers would have benefited from non-interventionist winemaking techniques and a dash of chemistry knowledge and scoopful of ethics. I guess they had not learnt—or heard—of the Austrian scandal.

~

Can wine be tested for adulteration?

YES.

There are now highly sophisticated detection techniques to determine if prohibited substances have been added to wine. As we have seen, unscrupulous winemakers may be tempted to alter wines to make them more appealing—not necessarily higher quality—to increase price, demand or sales or all and to give them an edge over the competition in a highly fragmented and competitive global market.

Most winemaking regions of the world have very strict rules and laws governing viticulture, winemaking, and wine marketing and sales, all in the interest of preserving authenticity, quality, and reputation. Most require growers and wineries to report harvest and production data such as yields, Brix (sugar) levels, varietals in blends, alcohol and so on. But with the advent of advanced analytical laboratory techniques, such as carbon and cesium dating, mass spectrometry (MS), gas chromatography (GS), high performance (or pressure) liquid chromatography (HPLC), and isotope ratios (IR) it is now possible to detect the presence and to accurately determine the concentration of the many compounds typically—or not typically—found in wine by comparing samples against a database of reference wines sampled from winemaking regions. Recent advances in hyphenated techniques are also proving very promising in authenticating wine—that is, for example, establishing provenance and even vintage year—and in tracing the winemaking process from grape growing to bottling. High-end producers are now embedding special data into bottle markings, corks, and labels to foil counterfeits.

Let's look at examples of adulteration and how it is detected.

Wine can be tested for adulteration by analyzing samples and looking for foreign substances—those that would not logically be found in wine. Additionally, if a parameter tests unusually high compared to a typical wine from the same region then further investigation may be warranted to ensure that the winemaker did not add any unauthorized substance if the region's winemaking laws do not allow such additions. For example, winemakers may decide to add sugar to the grape juice to increase the alcohol content of wine or add water to increase yield (although this reduces quality). Well, not all sugars are equal nor is water. These contain different isotopes of the central element. (Isotopes are different types of atoms of the same element but each having a different atomic mass and are denoted by their element name followed by the mass, e.g., carbon–12.) Sugar contains carbon–12 and carbon–13 isotopes while water contains oxygen–16 and oxygen–18 isotopes. Then, if isotope ratios are not within expected ranges it is likely that the wine has been tampered with.

Another example is the addition of strawberries or blueberries or other fruit or fruit flavoring to make that Pinot Noir or Cabernet Sauvignon a tad more fruit-forward. This can be easily detected by HPLC analysis and by comparing the anthocyanin profile to that of typical wines. Berry fruit or other fruit contain different anthocyanins (having different molecular structures) not normally found in wine.

Where it gets really interesting is in wines produced supposedly from one hundred percent *V. vinifera* cultivars but which contain some portion of wine from non-*vinifera* cultivars. *Vinifera* wines are the global standard both in terms of quality and price and in controlled appellations the practice of blending non-*vinifera* wine into *vinifera* wines is strictly prohibited. Certain *vinifera* varietals are also prohibited from being blended, however, this is very difficult to detect— authorities rely on "field" data to catch fraudsters. There is now a testing technique to determine if a non-*vinifera* wine has been blended into a *vinifera* wine thanks to some nifty glycoside molecular chemistry.

In wine, a glycoside is a flavonoid (a plant metabolite) and more specifically, an anthocyanin pigment molecule in reds with one sugar component—typically glucose—in its structure. In this case, the anthocyanin molecule is said to be monoglucosidic. A diglycoside is a flavonoid with two sugar (glucose) components and hence the anthocyanin molecule is said to be diglucosidic.

The interesting differentiating feature is that *V. vinifera* species are monoglucosidic whereas French hybrids and Native American grape species with some very few exceptions are diglucosidic. So by examining the molecular structure of anthocyanin pigment molecules in red wines, the presence of diglycosides confirms the presence of non-*vinifera* species in almost all cases.

Another technique to detect fraud is to test for the presence of methyl anthranilate (2-aminobenzoic acid methyl ester), an ester commonly used to manufacture synthetic perfumes and ointments which is found in significant quantities in *V. labrusca* varieties; it is also found in tiny quantities in Pinot Noir (a *V. vinifera*). The technique is used in certifying VQA wines where only *vinifera* cultivars are allowed. As the Ontario wine industry was transitioning from hybrids to *vinifera*s in the 1980s in its desire to make world-class wines, blending *labrusca* varieties was no longer allowed because they imparted an undesirable grapey aroma often but inaccurately described as foxy. Wine connoisseurs were simply not interested in the likes of Concord wines which many considered plain "awful."

And with advances in analysis techniques, we might soon be able to authenticate wine by comparing its DNA *fingerprints* against a databank to determine varietal(s) in the blend as well as provenance. A wine could then be profiled for varietal content (i.e., percentage of each grape variety used in the blend) and the exact vineyard where the grapes were sourced.

Grape DNA profiling, often referred to as *cultivar fingerprinting*, is much more advanced; it uses a DNA technique known as *polymerase chain reaction (PCR)* to amplify a specific region of a DNA strand, a technique often used in DNA replication applications. Wine DNA profiling still remains a bigger challenge. DNA fingerprints in wine are difficult to detect and analyze owing to the presence of yeast and bacterial DNA, DNA dilution, and wine chemistry—all of which add elements of analytical complexity.

~

How did Thomas Jefferson stir controversy in the wine world?

THOMAS JEFFERSON (1743–1826) did not stir controversy but his name and prized bottles of wine he once owned did cause a brouhaha and nasty lawsuits which spawned some serious sleuthing by prominent chemists and physicists.

Before he became the third President of the United States in 1801, Thomas Jefferson served as minister to France from 1785 to 1789 where he became fond of French wine but only the best wines, notably those from Château Lafite—the Pauillac estate winery known today as Château Lafite-Rothschild and which achieved *Premier Cru* (First Growth) status along with four other Médoc *châteaux* in the famous Bordeaux Wine Official Classification of 1855—and Château d'Yquem of Sauternes, the one and (still) only *Premier Cru Supérieur* in the same classification for whites. The classification was based on how much a wine could fetch on the market which was directly related to the quality of wine. A classified wine with its estate's rich history would come to acquire immense prestige and mystique and still fetch head-spinning prices at auctions. Auction houses go through great length to verify provenance (namely, reputation of consignor and ownership track records) and authenticity of bottles. Surely anyone paying thousands or tens of thousands of dollars or more for a priceless bottle would want some guarantee of authenticity.

And so it was that the controversy began in 1985 when a bottle of 1787 Lafitte—as it was spelled back then—owned by Thomas Jefferson was consigned to London-based Christie's auction house. The bottle, which Malcolm Forbes' son successfully bid and bought for an unprecedented £105,000 (equivalent to $156,450), was believed to be authentic, especially that the initials "Th. J." were engraved on the glass although the bottle had an uncharacteristically high fill level or what is known as *ullage* in wine-speak. (Bottles with low ullage may indicate that a wine is oxidized and well past its drinking prime and perhaps undrinkable and would therefore command

One of the famed, albeit controversial, bottle of 1787 Lafitte with Thomas Jefferson's initials.

a considerably lower price. Some deep-pocketed châteaux with a reputation to match have been known to offer a re-corking service to serious collectors. Each bottle is topped up to a high fill level and re-corked with a new cork.) Many were skeptical, and the historical sale was to ignite a series of events—some claimed fraud—that questioned and challenged the authenticity of any Thomas Jefferson bottles that still existed. Hollywood could not have scripted a more dramatic mystery and story which still linger on a quarter of a century later.

At the center of the storm was Meinhard Görke, a German rare-wine collector best known under the alias Hardy Rodenstock who was the only link to several other bottles of alleged counterfeit 1787 Lafitte and other late-eighteenth-century wines.

The challenge for the FBI, forensic and wine experts who were brought in to investigate the matter was really *how* to authenticate a two-hundred-year-old bottle.

What could it be compared to? How could the wine be tested without opening the bottle which would otherwise completely depreciate in value?

The challenge was submitted to German chemists and physicists for forensic analysis to determine the age of the wine. One test which required opening a bottle used thermoluminescence to date the sediment. It would measure the radiation level of isotopes in the sediment and comparing it to a database of levels recorded around the world and provide some indication of where and when the wine originated. The energy in the sediment reflects the naturally absorbed energy in vines which does not change as the grapes and juice are transformed into wine. The complex test concluded that the bottle originated sometime between the late seventeenth and mid- to late-nineteenth centuries, and therefore, that it was *possibly* legitimate and authentic. But as other tests were performed on the wine in the ongoing investigation with conflicting results and conclusions, suspicion grew about the bottle's authenticity. According to Benjamin Wallace in *The Billionaire's Vinegar*, carbon dating tests (these can date materials based on the measured level of radioactive decay of carbon isotopes), one of which was an accelerator mass spectrometry analysis performed at the University of Toronto concluded that the wine was from the early 1960s or late 1970s.

How could there be such a disparity between the estimated age of the wine and its sediment? Could the wine and bottle have been tempered? Even tests performed as recently as in 2005 using isotope cesium-137 dating were inconclusive. Cesium-137, according to Wallace, "didn't exist in nature in significant concentrations prior to the first hydrogen bomb test, in 1952."

As forgery in wine was becoming rampant it spawned worldwide criminal investigations lead by Scotland Yard and the FBI. The most intriguing investigation was that surrounding a lawsuit launched in 2006 by billionaire collector William Koch against Rodenstock. Koch claimed that four Jefferson bottles—the famous 1787 Lafitte, a 1784 Lafitte, and a 1784 and 1787 Château Branne-Mouton (now Château Mouton Rothschild)—for which he reportedly paid $500,000, were fakes. Needless to say, the whole episode and mystery turned into a legal wrangle as each successive test and defense argument contradicted earlier findings. Perhaps the most damaging argument against Rodenstock, who to this day still will not reveal his source or provenance except to say that they "come from a walled up cellar in Paris," was that of an expert's analysis which determined that the method used to engrave Thomas Jefferson's initials on the bottle was not the work of a tool from that era.

Can Rodenstock ever be exonerated of the allegations? Based on the complexity of the matter and lack of tangible and conclusive scientific evidence, perhaps not. But new research on dating vintage bottles at the *Centre national de la recherche scientifique (CNRS)* in Paris, France might pave the way for future work to build on. In September 2008, the CNRS in cooperation with the Antique Wine Company, a London-based purveyor of fine wines who also had connections to the Jefferson case announced that they could authenticate and date glass by placing the bottles under high energy ion beams propelled by a particle accelerator. X rays emitted from bottles are analyzed and compared to quantum data from prior collection tests. But here again, the database only contains information for wine bottles dating back to the nineteenth century. That must surely be good news for Rodenstock, and so the mystery lingers on.

∼

Epilogue

∼

So WHAT DOES SCIENTIFIC research and development have in store for the wine industry? What can we expect to see in the next decade or two, or more?

First and foremost, we can expect medical researchers to zero in on the benefits of red wine consumptions by establishing an unequivocal cause-and-effect relationship between wine constituents and health benefits. Hopefully, this will encourage the population to incorporate wine as part of everyday meals and a healthier lifestyle and that wine becomes accepted as a food. That means that the nutrition and health czars governing public policies develop more informative guidelines to allow wine producers to state nutritional facts and make substantive health claims on labels. Surely it will be a tough balancing act with social responsibility tipping the scale heavily. But the long-term health benefits of responsible, moderate drinking will surely reduce the existing heavy burden on our health care systems.

Secondly, advancements in the science of enology will help winemakers better understand the chemistry of wine and what makes a good wine so that we can implement better viticultural and winemaking methods. The primary objectives of good winemaking are to make better and better wines and reduce the occurrence of faults. Unfortunately, some of these changes enabled by science will rub traditionalists the wrong way, but we need to circumvent tradition if we are to improve on the product.

Thirdly, wine collectors and auction houses will start breathing a little easier with the introduction of new technologies developed to stymie counterfeit wines in the ultra-premium wine market. Top producers have already started, for example, etching bottles with codes that can be verified for authenticity against their database. Other interesting technologies being introduced include three-dimensional holographs on labels and DNA fingerprints and Radio-Frequency Identification (RFID) imbedded in labels as well as the use of Mass Spectrometry (MS).

Fingerprinting—a technology already in use in the pharmaceutical industry—imbeds a wine's natural component into the label for which its DNA can then be traced back to the producer's database or compared to authenticated bottles.

RFID technology too has been already been deployed, not only to thwart counterfeits but also for improved point-of-sale marketing. For example, wine consumers can scan the label on a bottle at the supermarket using a cell phone equipped with a camera to link to the producer's database to get information such as wine and food pairing—how clever!

Now, MS can be further used to authenticate the wine by actually testing the product *inside* the bottle although this is often not desirable, for example, for auction houses unless you intend to drink the wine. According to *Wine Spectator*, "[c]ompounds in a vaporized wine sample [can be] analyzed to determine the age of the barrel it was in. Factors such as climate change and lichen growth impact certain chemicals into the forests where barrels are sourced. Those chemicals are transferred to the wine. Scientists check to see if the barrels are younger than the stated age of the wine."

Interesting science!

Let's all raise a glass of (red) wine in the name of scientific research and healthy living.

References

Bamforth, Charles W. *Food, Fermentation and Micro-organisms.* Oxford, UK: Blackwell Science Ltd (Blackwell Publishing), 2005.

Baxter, Richard A., M.D. *Age Gets Better with Wine: New Science for a Healthier, Better and Longer Life.* Second Edition. South San Francisco, CA: The Wine Appreciation Guild, 2009.

Beekman Wines & Liquors. "Champagne – How Many Bubbles?" http://www.beekmanwine.com/prevtopam.htm/.

Berger, Ralf Günter, Dr., ed. *Flavours and Fragrances: Chemistry, Bioprocessing and Sustainability.* Heidelberg, Germany: Springer-Verlag Berlin Heidelberg, Springer Science+Business Media LLC, 2007.

Botezatu, A. and Pickering, G.J. (2009). *Ladybug (Coccinellidae) taint in wine.* IN Reynolds, A. G. Understanding and Managing Wine Quality and Safety. Woodhead Publishing Limited, Cambridge, U.K. (submitted).

Boulton, Roger B., Vernon L. Singleton, Linda F. Bisson, and Ralph E. Kunkee. *Principles and Practices of Winemaking.* New York, NY: Chapman & Hall, International Thomson Publishing, 1996.

Canada Green Building Council (CaGBC). *LEED Canada.* http://www.cagbc.org/leed/what/index.php/.

Catania Wine Enhancer. *Reduce Tannins and Red Wine Headaches, Improves Flavor.* http://www.lifeforceenhancements.com/.

Center for Science in the Public Interest. "TTB's New Guidelines Doom Health Claims for Labels and Advertising." *Alcohol Policies Project: Advocacy for the Prevention of Alcohol Problems.* http://www.cspinet.org/booze/TTBHealthLabel.htm/.

Chaboussou, Francis. *Healthy Crops: A New Agricultural Revolution.* Translated by Mark Sydenham, Grover Foley, and Helena Paul. Charlbury, UK: Jon Carpenter Publishing, 2004.

Chèze, Catherine, Joseph Vercauteren, and Robert Verpoorte, eds. *Polyphenols, Wine and Health – Proceedings of the Phytochemical Society of Europe, Bordeaux, France, 14th-16th April, 1999.* Dordrecht, The Netherlands: Kluwer Academic Publishers, 2001.

Clarke, Oz, and Margaret Rand. *Oz Clarke's Encyclopedia of Grapes: A Comprehensive Guide to Varieties and Flavors.* New York, NY: Harcourt, Inc., 2001.

Clarke, Ronald J., and Jokie Bakker. *Wine Flavour Chemistry.* Oxford, UK: Blackwell Publishing Ltd., 2004.

Corder, Roger. *The Red Wine Diet: Drink wine every day and live a long and healthy life.* New York, NY: Avery, Penguin Group (USA), Inc., 2007.

Costello, Peter, Dr., "The Chemistry of Malolactic Fermentation." *Malolactic Fermentation in Wine.* Lallemand Inc. (2005): 4:1-9.

Das, Dipak K., and Fulvio Ursini. *Alcohol and Wine in Health and Disease.* New York, NY: The New York Academy of Sciences, 2002.

Department of Treasury – Alcohol and Tobacco and Trade Bureau. *27 CFR Parts 4, 5, and 7: Health Claims and Other Health-Related Statements in the Labeling and Advertising of Alcohol Beverages (99R–199P); Final Rule.* Federal Register 27 CFR Parts 4, 5 and 7, TTB T.D.-1; ATF Notice Nos. 884, 892, and 896. (March 3, 2003). http://www.ttb.gov/regulations/ttb_td01.pdf/.

Ebeler, Susan E., Gary R. Takeoka, and Peter Winterhalter, eds. *Authentication of Food and Wine.* Washington, DC: American Chemical Society, 2007.

Emsley, John. *Molecules at an Exhibition: The Science of Everyday Life.* Oxford, UK: Oxford University Press, 1998.

Fenster, Ariel, Dr., *L'agriculture biodynamique.* Montréal, QC : Organisation pour la science et la société de l'Université McGill, 2003.

Flamini, Riccardo, ed. *Hyphenated Techniques in Grape and Wine Chemistry.* West Sussex, England: John Wiley & Sons, Ltd., 2008.

Flamini, Riccardo, and Pietro Traldi. *Mass Spectrometry in Grape and Wine Chemistry.* Hoboken, NJ: John Wiley & Sons, Ltd., 2010.

Ford, Gene A. *The Science of Healthy Drinking.* South San Francisco, CA: The Wine Appreciation Guild, 2003.

Frank, Mitch. "Harnessing Wine's Healing Powers." *Wine Spectator,* Vol. 34, No. 2 (May 31, 2009): 54–8.

Franson, Paul. "To Blow Up or Down? Inverted sink fans offer alternative form of frost protection." *Wines & Vines,* Vol. 90, No. 12 (December 2009): 32–5.

Fraser, Hugh, Ken Slingerland, Kevin Ker, K. Helen Fisher, and Ryan Brewster. *Reducing Cold Injury to Grapes Through the Use of Wind Machines – Final Report:CanAdvance Project # ADV – 161; Nov. 2005 – Nov. 2009.* Ontario: December 2009.

Fugelsang, Kenneth C., and Charles G. Edwards. *Wine Microbiology: Practical Applications and Procedures.* Second Edition. New York, NY: Springer Science+Business Media LLC, 2007.

Galet, Pierre. *Practical Ampelography: Grapevine Identification.* Translated and adapted by Lucie T. Morton. London, England: Comstock Publishing Associates and Cornell University Press, 1979.

Goode, Jamie. *The Science of Wine: From Vine to Glass.* Berkeley, CA: University of California Press, 2005.

Gove, Philip Babcock, Ph. D., and the Merriam-Webster Editorial Staff, eds. *Webster's Third New International Dictionary of the English Language, Unabridged.* Springfield, MA: Merriam-Webster Inc., 2002.

Grainger, Keith. *Wine Quality: Tasting and Selection.* West Sussex, UK: Wiley-Blackwell, John Wiley & Sons, Ltd., 2009.

Hallgarten, Fritz. *Wine Scandal: Blows the lid off the shocking practices of the wine trade.* London, England: Sphere Books Limited, 1986.

Hartel, Richard W., and Annakate Hartel. *Food Bites: The Science of the Foods We Eat.* New York, NY: Springer Science+Business Media LLC, Copernicus Books, 2008.

Hartley, Andy. "The Effect of Ultraviolet Light on Wine Quality." *Waste & Resources Action Programme.* (May 2008). http://www.wrap.org.uk/downloads/UV_wine_quaquaq_May_08.41a7e00bl.5388.pdf/.

Health Canada. *Water Quality and Health - Antimony: Exposure.* Date Modified: 2008-01-07. http://www.hc-sc.gc.ca/ewh-semt/pubs/water-eau/antimony-antimoine/exposure-expositions-eng.php/

Intergovernmental Panel on Climate Change (IPCC). http://www.ipcc.ch/.

IPCC, 2007: Summary for Policymakers. In: *Climate Change 2007: The Physical Science Basis. Contribution of Working Group I to the Fourth Assessment Report of the Intergovernmental Panel on Climate Change* [Solomon, S., D. Qin, M. Manning, Z. Chen, M. Marquis, K.B. Averyt, M.Tignor and H.L. Miller (eds.)].

Cambridge University Press, Cambridge, United Kingdom and New York, NY, USA.

Isaacs, Rufus, Annemiek Schilder, Tom Zabadal, and Tim Weigle, eds. *A Pocket Guide for Grape IPM Scouting in the North Central and Eastern United States*. East Lansing, MI: Michigan State University Extension, 2007.

Jackson, David, and Danny Schuster. *The Production of Grapes & Wine in Cool Climates*. Aoteroa, New Zealand: Gypsum Press and Daphne Brasell Associates Ltd., 2001.

Jackson, Ronald S. *Wine Science: Principles and Applications*. Third Edition. Burlington, MA: Elsevier Inc., Academic Press, 2008.

Joly, Nicolas. *BioDynamic Wine Demystified*. South San Francisco, CA: The Wine Appreciation Guild, 2008.

Keefe, Patrick Radden. "The Jefferson Bottles: How could one collector find so much rare fine wine?" *The New Yorker*. (September 3, 2007). http://www.newyorker.com/reporting/2007/09/03/070903fa_fact_keefe?currentPage=all/.

Klem, Bernard. *WineSpeak: A vinous thesaurus of (gasp!) 36,975 wine tasting descriptors. Who knew?*. Stamford, CT: Wine*Speak* Press LLC, 2009.

Komaroff, Anthony L., M.D., ed. *Harvard Medical School Family Health Guide*. New York, NY: Free Press, Simon & Schuster, Inc., 2005.

König, Helmut, Gottfried Unden, and Jürgen Fröhlich, eds. *Biology of Microorganisms on Grapes, in Must and in Wine*. Heidelberg, Germany: Springer-Verlag Berlin Heidelberg, 2009.

Kramer, Matt. *Making Sense of Wine*. Revised & Updated Edition of the Wine Classic. Philadelphia, PA: Running Press Book Publishers, 2003.

Lewis, Richard J., Sr., *Hawley's Condensed Chemical Dictionary*. Fifteenth Edition. Hoboken, NJ: John Wiley & Sons, Inc., 2007.

Liger-Belair, Gérard. *Uncorked: The Science of Champagne*. Princeton, NJ : Princeton University Press, 2004.

Liger-Belair, Gérard, Clara Cilindre, Régis D. Gougeon, Marianna Lucio, Istvan Gebefügi, Philippe Jeandet, and Philippe Schmitt-Kopplin. "Unraveling different chemical fingerprints between a champagne wine and its aerosols." *Proceedings of the National Academy of Sciences of the United States of America*. Vol. 106, No. 39 (September 29, 2009). http://www.pnas.org/content/106/

39/16545.full.pdf+html?sid=30ba8af6-d935-495a-8f0c-4e33d8472dfb/.

Loubère, Leo A., *The Red and the White: The History of Wine in France and Italy in the Nineteenth Century*. Albany, NY: State University of New York Press, 1978.

Marcus, Kim, and Jacob Gaffney. "A User's Guide to Wine Science: Summaries of recent findings and what they mean for wine drinkers." *Wine Spectator*, Vol. 34, No. 2 (May 31, 2009): 48–9.

Margalit, Yair, Ph.D. James Crum, Ph.D., ed. *Concepts in Wine Chemistry*. New Edition. South San Francisco, CA: The Wine Appreciation Guild, 2004.

———. *Concepts in Wine Technology*. South San Francisco, CA: The Wine Appreciation Guild, 2004.

Markham, Dewey, Jr. *1855: A History of the Bordeaux Classification*. New York, NY: John Wiley & Sons, Inc., 1998.

Maroon, Joseph, M.D. *The Longevity Factor: How Resveratrol and Red Wine Activate Genes for a Longer and Healthier Life*. New York, NY: Atria Books, Simon & Schuster, Inc., 2009.

Martin, Narelle. *Sustainable Winemaking Ontario: An Environmental Charter for the Wine Industry*. St. Catharines, Ontario: Two Hemispheres Environmental Consulting Inc. and the Wine Council of Ontario, 2007.

Mendelson, Richard. *From Demon to Darling: A Legal History of Wine in America*. Berkeley, CA: University of California Press, 2009.

Miller, Tracy. "Women who drink two glasses of wine a day have better sex than non-drinkers: study." Daily News, NYDailyNews.com. (August 6, 2009). http://www.nydailynews.com/lifestyle/health/2009/08/06/2009-08-06_women_who_drink_two_glasses_of_wine_have_better_sex_than_nondrinkers_study.html/.

Moreno-Arribas, M. Victoria, M. Carmen Polo, eds. *Wine Chemistry and Biochemistry*. New York, NY: Springer Science+Business Media LLC, 2009.

Mullins, Michael G., Alain Bouquet, and Larry E. Willians. *Biology of the Grapevine*. Cambridge, UK: Cambridge University Press, 1992.

Myers, Richard L. *The 100 Most Important Chemical Compounds: A Reference Guide*. Westport, CT: Greenwood Press, Greenwood Publishing Group, Inc., 2007.

National Agricultural Library, The. "USDA National Nutrient Database for Standard Reference." US Department of Agricultural. http://www.nal.usda.gov/fnic/foodcomp/search/.

Nossiter, Jonathan. *Liquid Memory: Why Wine Matters*. New York, NY: Farrar, Straus and Giroux, 2009.

O'Byrne, Paul, ed. *Red Wine and Health*. New York, NY: Nova Science Publishers, Inc., 2009.

Olney, Richard. *Romanée-Conti: The World's Most Fabled Wine*. New York, NY: Rizzoli International Publications, Inc., 1995.

———. *Yquem*. Suisse: Flammarion. 1985.

O'Neil, Maryadele J., ed. *The Merck Index: An Encyclopedia of Chemicals, Drugs, and Biologicals*. Fourteenth Edition. Whitehouse Station, NJ: Merck Research Laboratories, 2006.

Ough, C. S., and M. A. Amerine. *Methods for Analysis of Musts and Wines*. New York, NY: John Wiley & Sons, Inc., 1988.

Pambianchi, Daniel. *Techniques in Home Winemaking: The Comprehensive Guide to Making Château-Style Wines*. Newly Revised and Expanded Edition. Montréal, QC: Véhicule Press, 2008.

———. *Kit Winemaking: The Illustrated Beginner's Guide to Making Wine from Concentrate*. Montréal, QC: Véhicule Press, 2009.

Parente, Matilde, MD., *Resveratrol: Living Long, Living Well*. Salt Lake City, UT: Woodland Publishing, 2009.

Parker, James N., M.D., and Philip M. Parker, Ph.D., eds. *Wine: A Medical Dictionary, Bibliography, and Annotated Research Guide to Internet References*. San Diego, CA: ICON Group International, Inc., 2003.

Parker, Robert M., Jr., *Parker's Wine Buyer's Guide*. Seventh Edition. New York, NY: Simon & Schuster, Inc., 2008.

Parker, Steve. *The Human Body Book*. New York, NY: DK Publishing, 2007.

Paul, Harry W., *Science, Vine and Wine in Modern France*. Cambridge, UK: Cambridge University Press, 1996.

Paull, John. "Trophobiosis Theory: A Pest Starves on a Healthy Plant." Elementals - Journal of Bio-Dynamics Tasmania 88 (2007): 20–4.

Perfect Sommelier. *The Perfect Sommelier Gives You Age, Aroma and Fruit*. http://www.perfectsommelier.com/.

Peynaud, Émile. *Connaissance et travail du vin*. Paris, France: Dunod, 1984.

————. *Knowing and Making Wine*. Translated by Alan Spencer. New York, NY: John Wiley & Sons, Inc., 1984.

————. *The Taste of Wine: The Art and Science of Wine Appreciation*. Translated by Michael Schuster. London, England: Macdonald & Co. (Publishers) Ltd, 1987.

Pickering, G. J. (2010). *Ladybug (Coccinellidae) taint in wine.* Joint Ontario Grape and Wine Research Cluster and Champagne-Ardenne Grape and Wine Cluster Workshop, Brock University, 22-24th February, 2010.

PubMed.gov. U.S. National Library of Medicine National Institutes of Health. http://www.ncbi.nlm.nih.gov/pubmed/.

Ribéreau-Gayon, P., D. Dubourdieu, B. Donèche, and A. Lonvaud. *Handbook of Enology: Volume 1 – The Microbiology of Wine and Vinifications*. Translated by Jeffrey M. Branco, Jr. Chichester, England: John Wiley & Sons Ltd., 2000.

Ribéreau-Gayon, P., Y. Glories, A. Maujean, and D. Dubourdieu. *Handbook of Enology: Volume 2 –The Chemistry of Wine, Stabilization and Treatments*. Translated by Aquitrad Traduction. Chichester, England: John Wiley & Sons Ltd., 2000.

Rieger, Ted. "RAVE Focuses on Flavor: Annual UC Davis Conference Highlights the Latest Research." *Vineyard and Winery Management*. Vol. 35, No. 4 (July/August 2009): 66–8.

Robinson, Jancis, ed. *The Oxford Companion to Wine*. Third Edition. Oxford, UK: Oxford University Press, 2006.

————. *Jancis Robinson's Wine Course*. New York, NY: Abbeville Press, 1995.

————. *How to Taste: A Guide to Enjoying Wine*. New York, NY: Simon & Schuster, Inc., 2000.

Sandler, Merton, and Roger Pinder, eds. *Wine: A Scientific Exploration*. Boca Raton, FL: CRC Press LLC, 2003.

Schuller, Dorit-Elisabeth. *Saccharomyces cerevisiae strains for winemaking: Molecular characterization and genetic diversity*. Saarbrüken, Germany: VDM Verlag Dr. Müller, 2009.

Seethaler, Sherry. *Lies, Damned Lies, and Science: How to Sort through the Noise around Global Warming, the Latest Health Claims, and Other Scientific Controversies*. Upper Saddle River, New Jersey: FT Press Science, 2009.

Shur Farms. http://shurfarms.com/.

Shwartz, Mark. "Global warming could harm U.S. wine, corn production, Stanford scientists say: Understanding how global warming altered the lifecycles of plants and animals in the past can provide important insights about the impact of climate change in the future, says Stanford scientist Noah Diffenbaugh. His research team is using recorded observations of natural events to generate 30-year computer forecasts of how U.S. wine and corn production could be affected by global warming." Stanford Report, December 16, 2009. http://news.stanford.edu/ news/2009/december14/global-warming-wine-121609.html/.

Smart, Lesley, ed. *Alcohol and Human Health*. Oxford, UK: Oxford University Press, 2007.

Taber, George M. *Judgment of Paris: California vs. France and the Historic 1976 Paris Tasting that Revolutionized Wine*. New York, NY: Scribner, 2005.

———. *To Cork or Not to Cork: Tradition, Romance, Science, and the Battle for the Wine Bottle*. New York, NY: Scribner, 2007.

This, Hervé. *Molecular Gastronomy: Exploring the Science of Flavor*. Translated by Malcolm B. DeBevoise. New York, NY: Columbia University Press, 2006.

Thomas, Robert B. *The 2009 Old Farmer's Almanac, Canadian Edition*. Dublin, NH: Yankee Publishing, 2008.

U.S. Department of Health and Human Services and U.S. Department of Agriculture. *Dietary Guidelines for Americans, 2005*. 6th Edition, Washington, DC: U.S. Government Printing Office, January 2005. http://www.health.gov/dietaryguidelines/ dga2005/document/default.htm/.

U.S. Green Building Council (USGBC). *LEED*. http://www.usgbc.org/ DisplayPage.aspx?CMSPageID=51.

USP – U.S. Pharmacopeia. http://www.usp.org/.

Vine, Richard P., Ellen M. Harkness, and Sally J. Linton. *Winemaking: From Grape Growing to Marketplace*. Second Edition. New York, NY: Springer Science+Business Media LLC, 2002.

Wallace, Benjamin. *The Billionaire's Vinegar: The Mystery of the World's Most Expensive Bottle of Wine*. New York, NY: Crown Publishers, Crown Publishing Group, Random House, Inc., 2008.

Waterhouse, Andrew L., and James A. Kennedy, eds. *Red Wine Color: Revealing the Mysteries*. Washington, DC: American Chemical Society, 2004.

Weed, Augustus. "The Fight Against Fakes: Concerned Producers Are Taking Steps to Protect Their Brands From Counterfeiters." *Wine Spectator*, Vol. 34, No. 12 (December 15, 2009): 66.

White, Robert E. *Understanding Vineyard Soils*. Oxford, UK: Oxford University Press, 2009.

Wikipedia: The Free Encyclopedia. http://en.wikipedia.org/wiki/Main_Page.

Wilson, James E. *Terroir: The Role of Geology, Climate, and Culture in the Making of French Wines*. Berkeley and San Francisco, CA: University of California Press and The Wine Appreciation Guild, 1998.

Wine Cellar Express. *Age your wine to perfection in minutes!* http://www.winecellarexpress.com/.

Wine Clip, The. *The Physics of Better Wine*. http://www.thewineclip.com/cgi-bin/category.cgi?category=tech_receiver/.

Wine Lovers Page. *30 Second Wine Advisor: Wine magnets and snake oil*. http://www.wineloverspage.com/wineadvisor1/tswa051128.phtml/.

Ziraldo, Donald, and Karl Kaiser. *Icewine: Extreme Winemaking*. Toronto, ON: Key Porter Books, 2007.

Zoecklein, Bruce W., Kenneth C. Fugelsang, Barry H. Gump, and Fred S. Nury. *Wine Analysis and Production*. Gaithersburg, MD: Aspen Publishers, Inc., 1999.

Index

Véhicule Press
www.vehiculepress.com